GREAT AMERICAN ENTREPRENEURS

Cornelius Vanderbilt

Railroad Tycoon

Cassandra Schumacher

Cavendish Square
New York

Published in 2020 by Cavendish Square Publishing, LLC
243 5th Avenue, Suite 136, New York, NY 10016

First Edition

Library of Congress Cataloging-in-Publication Data

Names: Schumacher, Cassandra, author.
Title: Cornelius Vanderbilt : railroad tycoon / Cassandra Schumacher.
Description: First edition. | New York : Cavendish Square, [2020] | Series: Great American entrepreneurs | Includes bibliographical references and index. | Audience: Grades 9-12. Identifiers: LCCN 2018047432 (print) | LCCN 2018048275 (ebook) | ISBN 9781502645418 (ebook) | ISBN 9781502645401 (library bound) | ISBN 9781502645395 (pbk.)
Subjects: LCSH: Vanderbilt, Cornelius, 1794-1877--Juvenile literature. | Industrialists--United States--Biography--Juvenile literature. | Businesspeople--United States--Biography--Juvenile literature. | Railroads--United States--History--19th century--Juvenile literature.
Classification: LCC CT275.V23 (ebook) | LCC CT275.V23 S38 2020 (print) | DDC 338.092 [B] --dc23
LC record available at https://lccn.loc.gov/2018047432

Editorial Director: David McNamara
Editor: Kristen Susienka
Copy Editor: Alex Tessman
Associate Art Director: Alan Sliwinski
Designer: Joseph Parenteau
Production Coordinator: Karol Szymczuk
Photo Research: J8 Media

The photographs in this book are used by permission and through the courtesy of: Cover Ian Dagnall/Alamy Stock Photo; p. 4 Felix LipovShutterstock.com; p. 7 Roger Viollet Collection/Getty Images; p. 8 Leemage/Universal Images Group/Getty Images; p. 14 George Rinhart/Corbis/Getty Images; p. 18 Stock Montage/Archive Photos/Getty Images; pp. 22-23 Smith Collection/Gado/Archive Photos/Getty Images; pp. 26, 54, 60 Everett Historical/Shutterstock.com; pp. 30-31 Universal History Archive/Universal Images Group/Getty Images; p. 33 http://biltmore.s3.amazonaws.com/mediakits/5857/painting_goingtotheopera6x4_large.jpg/Wikimedia/File:Vanderbilt family 1874a.jpg/CC0; p.36 Dr. RenShen/Wikimedia/File:Thomas Gibbons.png/by-SA/4.0; pp. 40, 98-99 Corbis Historical/Getty Images; p. 42 Library of Congress Prints and Photographs Division; p. 44 James Bard/The Athenaeum.org/Wikimedia/File:North Star(steam yacht 1852) by Bard.jpg/CC0; p.48 ART Collection/Alamy Stock Photo; p. 50 ©SZ Photo/Scherl/Bridgeman Images; pp. 62, 76-77 Library of Congress/Corbis Historical/Getty Images; p. 67 GraphicaArtis/Archive Photos/Getty Images; pp. 70-71 American Locomotive Company/LOC/Wikimedia/File:Commodore Vanderbilt Locomotive.jpg/CC0; p. 80 Collegiate Images/Getty Images; p. 82 Interim Archives/Archive Photos/Getty Images; p. 85 Kean Collection/Archive Photos/Getty Images; p. 87 De Agostini Picture Library/Getty Images; p. 90 Howell & Meyer, NY/Wikimedia/File:Cornelius Vanderbilt by Howell & Meyer.jpg/CC0; p. 92 Bettmann/Getty Images; pp. 104-105 Steve Proehl/Corbis Documentary/Getty Images.

Printed in the United States of America

CONTENTS

INTRODUCTION

The Commodore and His Feats

Standing at 6 feet 2 inches (188 centimeters) with a hearty, rugged complexion, Cornelius "Commodore" Vanderbilt was a formidable rival. In personal and professional circles, Vanderbilt's imposing figure was both feared and respected. Born of strong, Dutch American stock and raised poor on the shores of Staten Island, New York, Vanderbilt cut his teeth early on hard work. He liked racing horses and worked hard. With little formal education, grammar and penmanship that seemed nearly illiterate, and willingness to throw a punch when the situation called for it, he was not what anyone expected to be the next great American businessman.

Cornelius Vanderbilt is memorialized in this statue, which stands outside Grand Central Station in New York City.

A Head for Business

With a quick mind and a truly epic work ethic, Vanderbilt started amassing his fortune at a young age. He began a small ferrying business and became an entrepreneur in his own right by the age of sixteen.

Vanderbilt's ruthless business sense and impeccable timing of the markets continued into adulthood and made him one of America's first tycoons. During his professional career, Vanderbilt ruled the steamboat and railroad industries of New York. He was an incredibly accomplished businessman who managed to provide exactly what the public needed: fast transport at an affordable price. From the 1820s to the 1860s, Vanderbilt controlled the steamship industry around New York and came to own the largest steamship operation in the United States. The man essentially controlled the Hudson River by the end of the 1850s, and with that controlled access to one of America's most influential and valuable ports, New York City. Following that, at the age of seventy, he next conquered the railroad industry—buying different rail lines running in and out of New York and Chicago. He soon built an empire.

In both industries, the Commodore, as he was called, transported people and freight for prices far below the rates of his competitors. This tactic was meant to dwindle down competition and choke rivals out of business or force them into selling. Vanderbilt was a force unprecedented in business and fiercely competitive. With an unquenchable desire to achieve and make money, he let very little stand in the way of his success. For his efforts, Vanderbilt was incredibly and undeniably rich. At his death at the age of eighty-two, he was worth an incredible $100 million. Today, that would be worth more than $2 billion. Vanderbilt biographer T.J. Stiles notes

This image from 1857 shows Vanderbilt's ship the *Vanderbilt*. It illustrates the ship's massive steam-powered paddle wheel that propelled the boat forward.

that, had Vanderbilt liquidated his assets just prior to his death, one in every twenty dollars in rotation would have been his. He owned one-twentieth of all the money in the United States.

The Legacy

Clearly, Vanderbilt left a legacy on his death. The crown jewel in his empire was the Grand Central Depot in New York City, which would eventually become Grand Central Terminal. His business efforts contributed to the rise of New York City as a business hub, helped feed the American Stock Exchange, and created a shipping and rail system that would change America forever. Perhaps most influential of all, however, was that Vanderbilt made the mold for modern American businessmen.

The rise of Cornelius Vanderbilt was the birth of the first American business tycoon. Over the course of his life, he set the precedent for industrial titans who changed the face of the United States of America forever.

CHAPTER ONE

Full Steam Ahead

The seeds of Cornelius Vanderbilt's eventual rise were planted well before he was born. At the turn of the eighteenth century, the environment in America was changing. People embraced new technologies and opportunities. The nineteenth century was coming. It would mark a new era with great potential.

In the late eighteenth century, Americans had won their freedom from England, and the United States Constitution was ratified. The new nation was born into a changing world, and Vanderbilt followed suit. By 1794, Vanderbilt's birth year, industrialization was just beginning, starting with revolutions in technologies never seen before. Machines like the cotton gin were mechanizing business and making production a huge market.

Lucky for both the nation and Vanderbilt, each embraced the technological wave that would sweep them

This drawing shows inventor James Watt with his improved version of Thomas Newcomen's steam engine.

into the future and their prospective fortunes and power. The storm of industrialization that followed the rise of the cotton gin transformed American life and made the new nation the perfect place to raise a great thinker and an eventual American titan.

Forged in Steam

Though the Founding Fathers started the United States, England helped foster the spirit of what would truly make America a force to recon with globally. They planted the roots of one of America's greatest international assets, ingenuity. It was in Cornwall, England, that an ironmonger named Thomas Newcomen started the long path toward Vanderbilt's success with a mine pump more than eighty years before the Commodore was born. In 1698, inventor Thomas Savery patented a steam pump that helped move water out of the mines. Newcomen added to Savery's pump and made it the first steam-powered engine, patented in 1712.

The first steam engine used atmospheric pressure to create a vacuum in a cylinder that caused a piston to move. The changes in pressure from condensation in the vacuum moved the piston up and down and powered the engine. This engine allowed miners to move water out of mines and "worked at twelve strokes a minute, raising ten gallons [38 liters] of water from a depth of 156 feet [48 meters]—approximately 5.5 horse power."[1]

The machine was not particularly efficient, especially not by contemporary standards, but for the period it was revolutionary. It cut mining cost and time considerably. It was the beginning of a huge shift in culture and an influential step toward a changing world. With a steam-powered pump, the Industrial Revolution began.

HARNESSING THE POWER OF STEAM

In 1765, Scottish inventor James Watt took Newcomen's engine and again revolutionized it. The Watt steam engine used a separate condenser from the original model to trap more steam and, through that, harness more power. The machine did not need to cool down to move the piston. Being able to run hot, unlike previous models, which cooled between pumps, allowed the engine to run faster and more efficiently, and produce a maximum amount of power. According to engineer Henry Petroski, this meant that "Watt's earliest engines consumed only about half the fuel required previously to do the same amount of work."[2]

This model would be adapted and modified over the coming years to power more than just the mining pumps of Newcomen's original engine. There is little doubt that the invention of the steam engine was one of the most singularly important developments in industrial history. Man had learned to create and use his own power. Society would never be the same again.

Industrializing

As America rebelled against King George III's rule in the colonies, Britain saw a revolution of its own. The Industrial Revolution began to shift through British society, changing the way people worked and the tools they used. Where once manpower and domesticated animals completed daily tasks, machines gradually began to replace them, easing and expediting labor. Power and machines were slowly working their way into everyday life. The Industrial Revolution signaled movement from manual labor to industry, or the use of steam power (and eventually other power sources), machinery, and factories for mass production. It changed British society and ultimately the world in a truly monumental way, and impacted the development of the United States of America in the same fashion. Though the country had severed ties with the motherland in 1776, Great Britain's industrial methods were welcomed on the shores in a way that her ruling never would be again.

Textiles

One of the biggest impetuses of change to the young and budding American society came in the form of a British immigrant. English textile businessman Samuel Slater arrived in 1789 and started the industrial movement that would shape the United States irrevocably. Slater brought with him illegally memorized plans for textile factories popular in Britain. They became the model for industrialization in America.

Slater would come to be known as the "father of the American factory system." Using waterpower, Slater's model revolutionized the textile industry. Harnessing the power generated by moving water, captured by a waterwheel, Slater's mills made it so that cotton could be spun by powered machines at a significantly more efficient and higher speed than ever before in the United States. Human hands could not keep up with mechanized means. A formerly tedious and timely task became the work of machines rather than man, and the United States was able to begin to explore the concepts of factories and industry. It did not take long for waterways across the Northeast to be dotted with factories churning out fabric at an unprecedented rate. America had a taste for the speed that came with industry, and it wanted more.

One of the largest markets for steamships and eventually railroads would be textiles. Shipping cotton and cotton products was equally big business, one that Vanderbilt grabbed on to throughout his career. Essentially, textile manufacturing was the root of the modern United States economy. Historian Gene Dattle states that the cotton farmed by enslaved people "brought commercial ascendancy to New York City, was the driving force for territorial expansion in the Old Southwest and fostered trade between Europe and the United States."[3]

Classes

America industrialized over the next century. The new nation took the model that the British had been fostering for years and set it up on their shores. Strongly driven by those early textile interests, innovation took the form of inventions like James Hargreaves's spinning jenny (1764) and Eli Whitney's cotton gin (1794). The spinning jenny spun wool into yarn at a rate that no human could compete with, and the cotton gin easily removed cottonseeds from freshly picked cotton, thereby changing American industry and history.

Eli Whitney's cotton gin, pictured here, began mass production in the United States by increasing the speed that cotton could be processed. It also ensured the continuation of slavery in the United States well into the nineteenth century.

With the invention of the cotton gin, cotton farming became a huge cash crop in the South. This boost in cotton production encouraged the development of plantations and the use and abuse of enslaved people. Slave labor enabled plantation owners to have a workforce without paying their workers' wages, but slavery was also one of the greatest systems of human injustice to exist within the United States. People, specifically Africans and African Americans, were bought and sold as laborers. They were granted incredibly limited access to resources and were physically and emotionally abused, often for generations. They had no rights and were not paid for their enforced labor. As plantations rose in popularity, demand for slave labor increased as a direct result of the invention of the cotton gin. Treatment of enslaved people was inhumane, and just one example of how new inventions were shaping industry and changing human lives. It also showed the power of industrialization; it changed society dramatically and not always for the better. The United States class system became more defined.

Prior to industrialization, American colonists and citizens lived in a predominantly agricultural society. It was a farming economy where people produced the goods and resources they needed to survive. There was some social stratification—in other words, social classes and diversification in jobs. There were farmers and merchants, as well as upper-class citizens. The upper class consisted of truly wealthy people, such as plantation owners and businessmen. The lower classes were marked by manual labor and lower incomes. Industrialization magnified these differences and led to more defined classes. Manufacturing changed the job market and thereby changed the class structure of the United States.

It was during the Industrial Revolution that concepts like the poor and working classes really rose to prominence.

The middle and upper classes benefited from the changes in technology that came. Higher classes had enough resources and income to buy the textiles and own the businesses and factories that were producing new revenue and income. They had career options that paid well and were a part of the productivity boom that came with industrialization. The working class and poor were not so lucky; they became the factories' labor force.

Workdays for factory laborers included long hours with very little pay. The tasks were repetitive and monotonous. There were no labor laws to protect workers as there are today, and children as well as adults were put to work. The factory machines were often dangerous and did not have safety precautions. As the factories were designed to produce the highest payout with the cheapest expenses, they were built as a means of making money rather than for comfort and were often dark and dirty. The machines could also be dangerous. Loose clothing could catch on moving parts of machines, and machine operators could end up with horrible wounds or be killed if the machines pulled them in. In many situations, all members of the family—including women and children—would have to work to make enough for the family to survive.

The middle class in general grew because industrialization offered new opportunities for employment, such as shopkeepers and merchants. There were more goods to be sold, and more people could take jobs selling those goods and make a decent living. Furthermore, members of the middle class that owned factories were able to move into the upper class as demands for goods rose, and they made more money by filling those demands quickly. This created a sect of society for the newly rich, called the "nouveau riche."

As for the rich, they profited the most and got richer. People who owned businesses in trade and manufacturing had more markets to work in and were thereby able to make more money. The greater selection of goods as a result of manufacturing meant greater access to luxuries and goods, which meant an even higher quality of life.

Cities Rising

Industrialization was centered around urban areas, and it caused American cities to grow. New factories and job options drew workers from rural areas, and populations in cities gradually swelled. In 1760, New York City was home to 18,000 people. There were 33,131 people there in 1790. By 1810, there were 202,589 people living there.

The growth of cities and industrialization became a part of the United States' development and identity, so much so that geographer Peter G. Goheen says, "The growth of great cities and the industrialization of their economies were central themes of the nineteenth-century American experience in the decades after 1840."[4]

For Cornelius Vanderbilt's rise in the business world, the city of New York was specifically essential. As a port city, it allowed for the movement of goods by the fastest means possible: water routes. Shipping was profitable, and New York City would become one of the greatest shipping hubs in US history.

New York, New York

In the seventeenth century, New York City began as a Dutch settlement called New Amsterdam. It was lost to the British in 1664 and became New York. In the following two hundred years, it would have a huge political impact.

In this drawing, the first capitol building, Federal Hall in New York City, stands tall, a testament to the power and strength of this city as early as the late 1700s. It is no surprise that such a city would give rise to one of the most powerful men in America, Cornelius Vanderbilt, and his empire.

In the lead-up to the American Revolution, New York hosted the 1765 Stamp Act Congress, an important early meeting of representatives from different colonies to voice their frustrations with English taxation. During the revolutionary years, New York acted as a Loyalist stronghold for a large portion of the war. The positioning of New York in relation to the Hudson River and the Atlantic Ocean made it a valuable route for moving troops and supplies to the British army. Pivotal battles like the Battle of Saratoga, fought in 1777, were waged in New York State. The Battle of Saratoga in particular enabled the Americans to win the war because it led to a strategic alliance with France. Finally, at the close of the war, the British departure from New York in 1783 signaled the end of the British presence in America.

It made sense that after the American Revolution New York was named the country's capital under the Articles of Confederation. From 1785 to 1790, the city remained the capital until it moved to Philadelphia, Pennsylvania. After that, New York City would move toward being a business hub.

In May 1792, the New York Stock Exchange (NYSE) opened on Wall Street under the name of the Buttonwood Agreement. Eventually, the NYSE would become one of the most valuable and influential stock markets in the world, trading internationally and influencing the global economy. It would also become a keystone in Cornelius Vanderbilt's future railroad success. However, before any of that could take place, Vanderbilt harnessed the power of steam.

Steam on the Water

The penultimate piece of groundwork toward Cornelius Vanderbilt's empire was laid in 1785 when innovator John

Fitch began exploring the idea of the ship propelled by steam power. The first steamship was 45 feet (14 m) long and took its maiden journey down the Delaware River in 1787. The members of the Constitutional Convention watched as it sailed.

From there, Fitch would build more ships, and in August 1791, he was granted the patent for the first steamship. The steamship was a brilliant idea. Unfortunately for Fitch, he did not have the financial backing to make it hugely successful. His boats were expensive to build, and finding investors proved challenging. It would take another man, Robert Fulton, to find the value in steam and a way to make money with it rather than just spend money on it.

Fulton's Steamship

Robert Fulton was a painter-turned-inventor. When his paintings failed to be well received, Fulton began exploring mechanics and propulsion. He experimented with submarines and boat propulsion, creating plans that depicted large steam-powered, revolving paddles to move the boat along. His idea was a good one, and while in Europe, he met someone who wanted to use that idea—Robert Livingston.

Robert R. Livingston was a member of the committee that had drafted the Declaration of Independence, a lawyer to the Continental Congress, then minster to France, and would eventually hold a twenty-year monopoly on steamboat travel in New York. He had a vested interest in Fulton's boat.

The two met in Paris in 1803 and began to collaborate on a working model. Using large paddle wheels and a steam motor, they experimented until they found something that worked. Livingston extended his monopoly, and eventually Fulton returned to New York to construct a boat for him.

Robert Fulton's first steamship, the *Clermont*, depicted here, was created in 1807. It was one of the fastest ways to travel at the time of its construction.

Fulton's *Steamboat*, as he called it, was 150 feet (46 m) long and used a single cylinder condensing steam engine. There were large, 15-foot- (4.6 m) tall side paddle wheels that moved the boat forward. It was fueled by oak and pine and managed to run at nearly 4.7 miles per hour (7.6 kilometers per hour). The steamboat could travel from New York City to Albany, New York, in thirty-two hours. Traditional sailing vessels took four days to make that trip.

Over the coming months, Fulton continued to improve on his ship, and it was finally registered in 1808 as the *North River Steamboat of Clermont*, known later only as the *Clermont.* Livingston and Fulton launched a successful partnership. Steamships were officially on the Hudson River. The road was paved for the rise of the Commodore's shipping empire, but it was railroads that would truly change American commerce.

Engines on Land

Vanderbilt's final ticket to success came once again from Britain, this time by way of train. Railroads were another British triumph of the Industrial Revolution. British inventor George Stevenson experimented with the Newcomen steam engine at a young age and later John Blenkinsop invented a steam engine that attached to a cart to move coal out of mines. Stevenson would revolutionize the steam engine and increase the power, eventually creating an exhaust steam engine that used a chimney to bring in air to fuel the engine. He created the locomotive. Over the coming years, he would build more locomotives, and their popularity would boom.

The very first American railroad, the Baltimore and Ohio Railroad, broke ground on July 4, 1828. From there the industry blossomed. Railways connected distant cities and allowed people to travel at unprecedented speeds. Mercantile shipments and goods moved faster than ever. The American train industry was born, and the United States would never be the same. As economist Paul H. Cootner says, the role railroads played in the United States was "an epic role, involving enterprise on the grand scale, evoking heated passions."[5]

Those passions would lead to competition, Vanderbilt's favorite thing. The final piece had been laid on the way to making a millionaire—and the nation could never have expected what Vanderbilt would eventually do with railroads.

CHAPTER TWO

The Commodore

Cornelius Vanderbilt led an astounding life. He was born of old-school Dutch stock in Port Richmond on Staten Island, New York, and would come to be one of the wealthiest Americans in the history of the United States. His sharp mind and forceful nature combined with a fierce sense of personal competition made him a truly remarkable character. Biographer T.J. Stiles says, "Rumor and legend has it that he was involved in numerous fist fights, and … engaged in fist fights and won into his 50s."[1] He was not one to back down from a battle and gained many enemies.

Not everyone had a kind word for the Commodore, but no one could deny he was good at what he did—making money. A product of both his parents' hard work

Cornelius Vanderbilt was a stern, imposing man who never backed down from a fight. This portrait is one of the most common portraits of Vanderbilt and shows his serious and strong features.

and thriving in an age of innovation, Vanderbilt knew a good deal when he saw it and managed to read trends in economic markets remarkably well. Combined with an iron will and a shrewd mind for strategy, Cornelius Vanderbilt fashioned a transportation empire unlike anyone in the United States had before him, but before all that he was a poor boy on Staten Island toiling alongside his father.

Forging a Titan

Cornelius Vanderbilt was born on May 27, 1794, into a family structured on hard work. His great-great grandfather, Jan Aertsen Van Der Bilt, had immigrated in 1650 as an indentured servant. Perhaps originating from the Bildt or Bilt regions of Holland, hence "Van Der Bilt," the name would morph into "Vanderbilt" as a result of immigration and would later become iconic in American society, thanks to Jan's great-great grandson.

Cornelius Vanderbilt's parents were entrepreneurial and thrifty. His father farmed and ran a ferry service on New York's harbor. It was there that Vanderbilt became a boatman. At eleven years old, he dropped out of school to work with his father in the ferry business. Vanderbilt left the schoolroom able to read, but with nearly illegible penmanship and a tendency to spell words phonetically. What letters remain from Vanderbilt are peppered with misspellings and phonetic spellings. From his letters, historians assume he wrote the way he spoke. "Air" became "are" and he would add an "a" to verbs ending in "ing," like "awalking" or "agoing," as well as other interesting idiosyncrasies that made his speech and letter-writing distinct. He was only fundamentally literate, but he learned the lessons he truly needed for his future on the water with his father. Those skills would make him a millionaire.

While working with his father, Vanderbilt learned the value of hard work, that a ferryman could set his own price depending on how badly a person needed crossing, and the fundamental ideas of borrowing and lending money, as well as earning what you reap. He was entrusted by his father to make trips between Staten Island and New York City and was given the responsibility of managing cargo loads on the way to the docks. He was an important part of the family business in little to no time and carried a lot of responsibility for an eleven-year-old.

Vanderbilt's mother, Phebe Hand, also contributed to his early lessons. Writer Dorothy Kelly MacDowell describes Phebe as "strong of character and body … energetic, reliant, efficient, pious, and greatly loved by her family."[2] She is often credited with teaching her son the value of the dollar and shaping his business sense. She was especially respected by Vanderbilt and acted as his advisor well into his adulthood. She was known for being sensible and had money in her own right, independent of her husband. In fact, there is a story that says it was Phebe who gave Vanderbilt the loan that would fund his future empire.

According to legend, Phebe promised Vanderbilt a loan of $100 on May 1 of the year he turned sixteen. She said she would give him the money if he could plow a rough, rocky 8-acre (3-hectare) field by hand by his birthday. Vanderbilt worked diligently to meet the terms of the deal, and his mother gave him the loan. Vanderbilt used the money to purchase his first boat, a periauger, and went into the ferrying business for himself, taking people from Staten Island to New York City.

A periauger is a flat-bottomed boat with two sails. It usually has oars for rowing too. Vanderbilt's served him well. By the following year, Vanderbilt had managed to repay the loan and added an extra $1,000 to his family's income. Another

The War of 1812, depicted here in the Battle of New Orleans in 1815, offered Vanderbilt an opportunity to work government freight contracts that helped his ferrying business flourish even with the closing of the port.

version of events says that his first ship was loaned to him by his parents, and that he was allowed to keep half the profits from his efforts.

Regardless, sailing was hard work and honed strong muscles on his tall frame. He quickly gained a reputation as an efficient ferryman known for making safe passage of goods and people, even in rough waters. He added trade cargo when he could and took every opportunity to make a dollar when possible. It is said that Vanderbilt would sleep on his ship to be sure he never missed an opportunity at an odd job and a chance to make a dollar. From there, he would invest his money back into other moneymaking opportunities, buying partial ownership in other boats. In little time, he joined the ranks of a capitalist system.

The War of 1812

Vanderbilt had been in business for a couple years when America faced its first war as a country. Thought of by some as the "second revolution," the War of 1812 was a British effort to regain control of American interests. It was also a battle fought predominantly at sea, which offered Vanderbilt a unique business opportunity.

British ships were making freight deliveries between Staten Island and New York City challenging. Vanderbilt, however, picked up government contracts moving freight between the two areas while war raged. Even when the British closed the port and set up a blockade of American trade with France in 1813, Vanderbilt was able to prosper. He was operating within the port, which made him able to continue his business. He came out of the war wealthier and continued working toward another project, courting his future wife.

Marriage and Family

Cornelius Vanderbilt did not look far for a wife. Sophia Johnson was a close cousin also raised in Port Richmond. Vanderbilt's mother was quite worried that the close family ties would have a very negative effect on any children born of the union, but Vanderbilt insisted on Sophia. She was known to be beautiful, hardworking, and agreeable. She and Vanderbilt married in December 1813. Sophia was eighteen years old; Vanderbilt was nineteen. Their first child, Phebe, was born in the summer of 1814. Many more children would follow. Together Sophia and Vanderbilt had twelve children, eleven of whom survived into adulthood. Of their children, only three were boys, much to Vanderbilt's dissatisfaction.

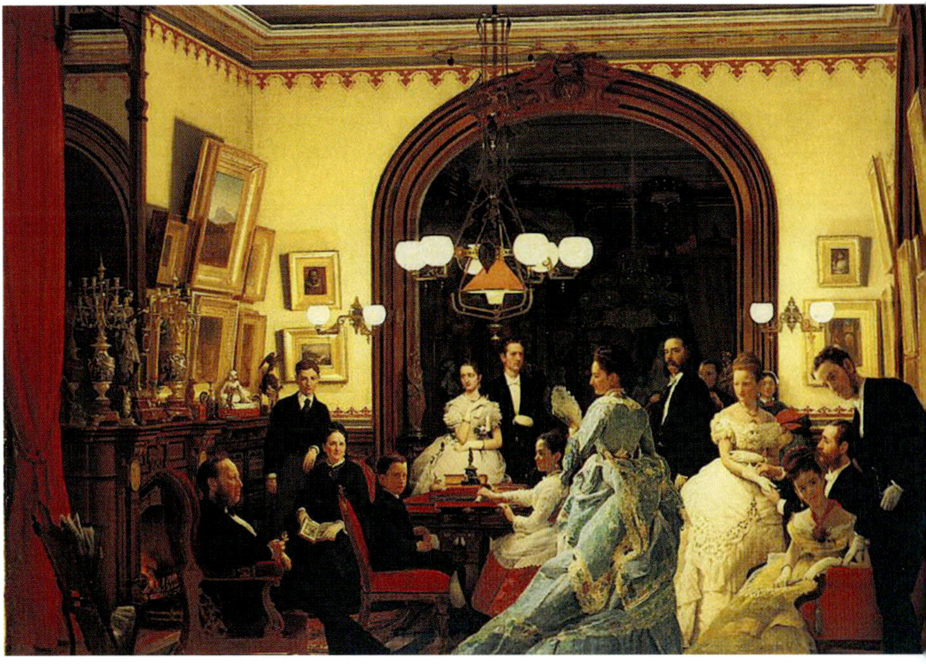

This 1874 painting by Seymour Guy shows the Vanderbilt family dressed in expensive finery waiting to see an opera. The large family only lived lavishly later in life.

It is important to note that though he was a wonderful businessman, he made a pretty deplorable husband and father. Most of his energy and nearly all of his money was poured into his business. The family lived frugally. In their first year of marriage, the Vanderbilts lived in a boarding house so that much of their income could be recycled back into business interests. The shipping business was so important to Vanderbilt that once the nickname "Commodore" caught on, even his children would refer to him by his honorary title.

Before all else Vanderbilt was a businessman. Family took a backseat to business interests. He worked long hours and left the children to Sophia. When he was around, Vanderbilt did not make much of a father or a husband. He is thought to have cheated rampantly on his wife and was known to be verbally abusive to both his spouse and children. He was also negligent with his children and had a noticeable favorite in his son George, whom he groomed to be the heir to his gradually growing shipping empire. Somewhat of a misogynist, Vanderbilt apparently took very little interest in his daughters.

What Vanderbilt lacked as a parent, Sophia well made up for. Her children remembered her with love and kindness. She was a good wife to Vanderbilt and lived within his very frugal lifestyle without complaint, never voicing concerns about his brashness or infidelities.

Vanderbilt ran roughshod over Sophia's calm and accepting nature and served his own purposes during their marriage. One particularly brutal example happened when Sophia was going through menopause. Her moods upset him, and during that time Vanderbilt was indulging in many outings with their governess. Likewise, Sophia didn't want to move to Manhattan with the family, which seemed inevitable. One day, after

Sophia returned from a trip to Canada, Vanderbilt had her institutionalized in an asylum. His children eventually forced him to bring her home, but this anecdote shows his indifference to her well being.

Vanderbilt would also institutionalize his second son and namesake, Cornelius Jeremiah Vanderbilt, whom he ridiculed for having depression and epilepsy. The institutionalization was in response to his son's gambling debt. Cornelius Jeremiah was deemed mentally sound and released, but this depicts Vanderbilt's handling of family issues. He was as ruthless with his family as he was in business.

On the Water

While Sophia worked at carrying and caring for their children, Vanderbilt pursued his first and deepest passion, business. He would spend several years investing in new boats and increasing the size of his fleet. In 1815, he was well on his way to having a formidable reputation in the shipping industry on the Hudson River. Well known for manning and captaining his own ships, he gained the nickname of "the Commodore," and it would stick with him for the rest of his life.

By 1817, Vanderbilt was only twenty-three years old, a reputable businessman, and had moved his family comfortably into the middle class. His shipping lines ran along the northeast and he had a steady stream of business that kept his ships stocked with freight, running up and down the coast. Vanderbilt, however, felt the changing tides in the air and on the water. Steamships were becoming more prevalent on the Hudson River as a part of the Livingston-Fulton monopoly on steam travel. The trends in business were changing and Vanderbilt had to decide if he was going to change with it.

Signing On with Steam

Steam was taking over the Hudson and shipping in New York. For Vanderbilt, the year 1818 opened the door to an unexpected opportunity in the form of Thomas Gibbons, a steamboat owner looking to compete in the Hudson River steamship market with his Union Line.

Gibbons called Vanderbilt in for a meeting, and Vanderbilt took an instant liking to him. After that meeting, he signed a contract with Gibbons. For someone as strong-willed and independent as Vanderbilt to work for someone else speaks of how much respect Vanderbilt had for the man, especially because Vanderbilt took a pay cut to work for him. It, however, was a well-timed offer on Gibbons's part. Vanderbilt was contemplating the roll that steamers would play in shipping and could see his traditional crafts being left in their wake. He was quick to liquidate his boats once he and Gibbons signed a contract.

Thomas Gibbons was a short, rotund man who owned the Union Line shipping company. He introduced Vanderbilt to steam-powered travel.

On June 26, 1818, Vanderbilt signed Gibbons's contract. It stated that he would be paid $60 a month (about $1,129 today) to captain Gibbons's steamship, *Mouse*. The ship would run between Elizabethtown, New Jersey, and Trenton, New Jersey, making a couple of stops along the way.

The change in Vanderbilt's employment also meant the Vanderbilts would move from a small apartment into a property owned by Gibbons. They got to live rent-free in an apartment above a tavern, in exchange for fixing the tavern up and turning it into a profitable business. The Vanderbilts would turn over 20 percent of the profits from the venture and were allowed to keep the rest. It was a formidable challenge that Sophia turned into a good venture. She renamed the business Bellona Hall. Thanks to her efforts, it became one of Gibbons's most valuable holdings on his Union Line.

The union was equally profitable for Gibbons on Vanderbilt's side of the deal, ferrying. Vanderbilt was a masterful captain, and his expertise was the true strength behind Gibbons's business. As time passed, Vanderbilt was running the *Mouse* diligently but eventually came up against a challenge. He was competing with Aaron Ogden's steamer line. Initially a partner with Gibbons, Ogden was now Gibbons's and Vanderbilt's fiercest competitor. It was hard to compete with his larger, more luxurious ship. Vanderbilt quickly convinced Gibbons to commission a larger boat, the *Bellona*, and took control of her construction. The new ship was larger. It had a copper engine and was designed with passenger comfort in mind. The line became a huge success with the introduction of the new ship.

Under Gibbons's tutelage, Vanderbilt's iron will and ruthless business methods fully formed. Vanderbilt used his strengths and fortitude to make Gibbons successful against competitors.

Furthermore, the two would end up in a pivotal Supreme Court case, *Gibbons v. Ogden*, that would impact monopolies in the United States for decades.

Gibbons v. Ogden

Working for Thomas Gibbons, Vanderbilt learned valuable lessons in law. Robert Livingston and partner Robert Fulton, through the state of New York, owned the right to a monopoly on steamboat navigation on the Hudson River. Aaron Ogden had purchased the right to run ships on the Hudson River from Livingston in 1815. Gibbons had not, but he started Vanderbilt running a line on the Hudson anyway. Vanderbilt would be arrested at times, but always managed to get out of it thanks to connections, even if the fines for violating the monopoly stood.

In 1818, Ogden ultimately sued Gibbons for attempting to compete with him on the line that he did not have the right to use, and won. Gibbons was ordered to cease operation. Gibbons and Vanderbilt refused to accept the ruling. Instead, they took the case to the Supreme Court. Gibbons had a federally issued government license that said he was allowed to operate in US coastal waters. He argued that ferrying passengers counted as interstate commerce and was therefore regulated by the Constitution and not the state government.

When the court finally heard the case, it was ground shaking in national business. On March 2, 1824, the court declared that the Livingston-Fulton monopoly was illegal because it restricted interstate commerce. It was declared illegal for states to pass legislation that restricted interstate commerce henceforth. Vanderbilt and Gibbons were free to keep running their ferry, and this opened the path for Vanderbilt to start his own line.

Friends to the End

Gibbons and Vanderbilt were a fierce team. The time working under Gibbons would help launch Vanderbilt's own success. The partnership was profitable for both parties, and Vanderbilt would come to respect Gibbons almost as a second father. The feelings were not extended to Gibbons's son William, however. Two years after the *Gibbons v. Ogden* decision, Gibbons passed away, leaving the line to his son, and things changed.

William took control in 1828 and changed the tone of Vanderbilt's employment. Vanderbilt did not have the respect for William that he had for the late Gibbons. Vanderbilt was forced to sever ties with Gibbons's line. William put the line up for sale at $400,000, a price Vanderbilt was not willing to pay. There was very little value in the Union Line without the Commodore's expertise and captaining. Vanderbilt let it be known to competitors that the sale of Union Line would also be the end of his work with the Union Line, thereby stripping the value of the sale without William Gibbons's knowledge. The line did not sell.

In this way, Thomas Gibbons's death signaled a pivotal moment for Vanderbilt. From briefly working with William, the Commodore took away a very valuable lesson that would drive his business dealings for the rest of his life. Vanderbilt biographer Edward J. Renehan Jr. says it best: "Never be a minion; always be an owner."[3]

Launching a Line

Cornelius Vanderbilt leaving the Union Line was the end of the Vanderbilts' life at the tavern, Bellona Hall. The family moved into a poor tenement building on the East River with

The Commodore's frugal nature had his family living in dirty, low-income housing to try to save money. Later in life, he would be less stringent, but he never lost his severity.

three bedrooms rented for $100 annually. It was small, dirty, and cramped. The Vanderbilts could have afforded better accommodations by this time, but Vanderbilt was incredibly frugal, and he was about to launch his own steamboat line at the age of thirty-five.

Vanderbilt's first steamship, the *Citizen*, launched in spring of 1829. By June of that year, William Gibbons was forced to sell the Union Line, without Vanderbilt's support, for significantly less than he had hoped. His line failed without Vanderbilt's expertise. In turn, Vanderbilt bought two ships from Gibbons, one of which was the *Bellona*. These three ships made up Vanderbilt's first personal shipping line, which he called the Dispatch Line. He did well in shipping.

It was also during this time that Vanderbilt experienced one of the greatest turning points in his life. On November 11, 1833, the era of the railroad was beginning, and Vanderbilt saw the value of the new and fast means of travel. There was money to be made in railroads. Looking to explore this new venture, Vanderbilt took a rail trip from Amboy, New Jersey, to Philadelphia, Pennsylvania.

The train ran at 25 miles per hour (40 kmh), an incredible speed. Unfortunately, this trip never made its destination. While passing Hightstown, an axel broke on one of the cars, causing the train to derail. The accident marked the first railroad accident with fatalities in United States history. Two people were killed, and Vanderbilt was among the wounded. The Commodore had broken three ribs and punctured a lung. It is rumored that Vanderbilt vowed to never ride another train again, but the future held a different plan.

First, however, he would explore American international shipping markets.

Shipping Life

The following twenty years would be filled with choking out competitors when the need demanded and viciously slashing prices to achieve the means he wanted. Vanderbilt was ruthless when it came to business. His fortitude was legendary. Competitors were afraid to go up against him because he was essentially relentless. The man did not like to lose, and he had the skill to stand against a competitor and win. Vanderbilt

THE JACKSONIAN IDEOLOGY AND VANDERBILT

Andrew Jackson was president during the Commodore's rise. Considered one of America's most controversial leaders, he was responsible for abuses against Native people, most notably the forced relocation of Native populations on the Trail of Tears. He battled the National Bank, and he used the "spoil system" and nepotism to replace political offices with friends and supporters. He was also a president to the people. Known as "Old Hickory" and a war hero, he campaigned against elitist members of society and appealed to the general public with his brash manners and newly formed Democratic Party.

Andrew Jackson was the seventh president of the United States, and arguably one of the most contentious. He and Vanderbilt had a great deal in common ideologically.

As Vanderbilt biographer T.J. Stiles states, "[Vanderbilt] epitomized the Jacksonian ideal of every man being free to compete and rise on his merits."[4] The populist mentality that got Jackson elected and made him popular to supporters was the same model Vanderbilt used to garner support for his shipping and rail lines. Both sold the idea of being on the people's side. Jackson attacked the National Bank; Vanderbilt slashed prices. They gave the people what they wanted when the competitors would not or could not afford to do the same. As Vanderbilt would famously say, "I have always served the public to the best of my ability. Why? Because, like every other man, it is to my interest to do so."[5]

crafted an empire around that business methodology, often leaving competitors bitter and broken in his wake.

By 1840, Vanderbilt was a millionaire and had a huge fleet of steamboats running in American waters. When the 1850s saw the California gold rush, Vanderbilt responded to public need and provided a steamer line from New York to San Francisco. It was the fastest route to California by way of Nicaragua and turned him a very hefty profit. His annual earnings from that line alone surpassed $1 million (over $30 million today) a year.

High Society

One market was a true challenge to Vanderbilt—high society. With his brashness, ineloquent speech, and rough-edged manner, Vanderbilt was not a "man about town." He did not have the dignified air of old money and inheritance but instead the forceful nature of a successful ship's captain and intense businessman. Despite this, Vanderbilt wanted the acceptance of the upper crust of society and to be seen as "a man of honor and integrity" among business associates and respected for his successes.

Doors in high society, however, remained closed to him and his family. They had the money but not the class. By the 1840s, the Vanderbilts had left behind their tenement apartment and were living in a newly built, large brick home at 10 Washington Place in Manhattan, but earning a place in society required more than just a nice home and wealth.

They were eventually accepted by the newly wealthy and found their place among them, but as for old families, the Vanderbilts' money was not enough to buy their way into the ballrooms of high society. New money was treated differently

Vanderbilt's private yacht, the *North Star*, was a massive, lavish ship that the Vanderbilt family used to take a European tour.

from established families, and it would take another generation before the Vanderbilts were accepted in society's upper echelons. Vanderbilt would find his place in society through the Union Club and the Manhattan Club in New York. There he would make connections with other powerful men that motivated him and would benefit him during his railroad years.

Through those years, Vanderbilt remained fabulously wealthy. In 1853, he ordered the construction of a large and lavish yacht. Known as the *North Star*, the yacht was the largest in existence at the time and was used to carry the entire

Vanderbilt family on a tour of Europe. According to an article in *Vanderbilt Magazine*, the trip cost somewhere around $500,000 (over $15 million today).

Vanderbilt and the Civil War

Vanderbilt was a self-serving businessman. He worked for his own interests, but at heart he was also a deeply dedicated patriot. When the country broke out in civil war in 1861, Vanderbilt was quick to offer aid. He provided the *Vanderbilt*, his fastest steamship—in fact, it was the fastest steamship in America at the time—for the Union's use during the war effort. The offer was largely ignored until March 17, 1862. The Union's naval efforts were failing, and its ships were taking a beating. Vanderbilt met with the United States secretary of war, Edwin Stanton, and the president of the United States, Abraham Lincoln. They needed a ship that could stop or sink the Confederates' *Merrimack*. Vanderbilt was confident that his *Vanderbilt* could accomplish the task.

The president offered to rent or buy the ship and asked Vanderbilt for his price. Vanderbilt was insulted that they would assume he would charge and insisted on donating the ship to the cause.

Vanderbilt prepared the ship, and Commodore Louis Goldsborough took her into battle. It was a $1 million donation to the war effort and left the Confederates shaken to hear of the ship.

The *Vanderbilt* never saw formal battle, though, for the Confederates were unwilling to risk the *Merrimack* against the Commodore's well-equipped ship. The threat of her, combined with the other Union ships, led to an important Confederate retreat, however.

The Confederates also began targeting Vanderbilt's California shipping line in an attempt to weaken him. Vanderbilt merely reinforced the protections on his shipping vessels. Instead of being cowed, he continued to offer support by donating another ship to the Union, though this time, the venture failed.

Ultimately, Vanderbilt's support of the Union forces was significant and impactful. In 1864, he received a Congressional gold medal, the highest honor granted to a civilian, for his support of the army and the donation of his ships.

After the War

Rebuilding the nation after the Civil War was slow. Vanderbilt had suffered his own losses. George, the heir apparent, had not survived the war. He had contracted a lung infection and died. Vanderbilt was forced to accept William, his far less fit son, as his future heir. It also marked the end of Vanderbilt shipping interests.

In 1864, Commodore Vanderbilt decided to retire from shipping. The tides were changing again, and railroads were impossible to ignore. The seaman was taking a turn on dry land. At seventy years old and worth $30 million (over $454 million in 2018), Vanderbilt was entering the railroad industry.

This was not the only large change in the Vanderbilt household. Vanderbilt and Sophia had grown increasingly farther apart and had spent many years living relatively separately. He continued to be unfaithful, and there is some evidence that it was his infidelities that led to her demise. During their marriage, Sophia possibly contracted syphilis from her husband, who more than likely contracted it during one of his affairs. In 1868, Sophia Vanderbilt died of a stroke.

The death of Vanderbilt's wife increased his interests in the occult and spiritualism. He would consult spiritual physicians to combat pains and illnesses in his aging body, as well as to communicate with his deceased mother, son, and wife. He attended séances and was interested in interacting with the dead. It was during this time that he would meet his next wife.

Vanderbilt would marry yet another cousin a year after Sophia's death, Frank Armstrong Crawford. She was decades younger than Vanderbilt when they eloped in 1869. In fact, she was younger than some of his children. There was more than a thirty-year age difference between her and her husband. Frank, a pious woman, worked hard to keep Vanderbilt on track. She tried to lead him away from the spiritualists he gravitated to after Sophia's death. It was also through Frank and her quest to improve and save her husband's soul that Vanderbilt began to reach out to the South. He would eventually help mend ties sorely frayed between the two regions that had been divided throughout the war. In March 1873, Vanderbilt made a $1 million (over $19 million in 2018) donation to the Central University in Tennessee at the urging of his young wife. It would be the only philanthropic contribution Vanderbilt ever made, but it would be a lasting one. Central University would be renamed Vanderbilt University, and it remains a top college in the twenty-first century.

The Final Years

Vanderbilt spent the end of his life doing what he did best, making money. The Commodore tackled railroads with the same tenacity and vigor that he brought to shipping. While some competitors thought him old and haggard, Vanderbilt

Frank Armstrong Crawford Vanderbilt was a dignified, young woman who was much respected by Vanderbilt and impacted his business decisions and charitable giving later in life.

was quick to show them the errors of their ways. He was still a captain of industry.

With the railroads, Vanderbilt changed tactics and bought struggling rails until he amassed the longest rail line between New York City and Chicago. The hub of his empire was the massive construction of a huge rail station in the heart of the now booming New York City. In 1871, Vanderbilt opened the Grand Central Depot, which would eventually become Grand Central Terminal. The project cost $6.4 million (over $125 million in 2018).

Those were the waning years of Vanderbilt's life. In 1876, he fell ill and slowly declined over several months. Due to his singular level of tycoon celebrity, the media tracked his progress and reported regularly on his health and well being.

In that way, Vanderbilt's final months were spent living with very public illnesses.

During this time, Vanderbilt received visitors as his health fluctuated, but he never managed to fully improve. Months of complications in his digestive tract and heart were too much in the end. It is possible that syphilis contributed to his death, the very illness that affected his first wife, though that is debated by historians.

Frank Vanderbilt painstakingly tracked her husband's last weeks in her diary, and Vanderbilt managed to get his affairs in order and share some meaningful moments with his beloved wife. Ultimately, his final days were likely spent delirious and unconscious. On January 4, 1877, Commodore Cornelius Vanderbilt died; he was eighty-two years old.

STANDARD PUSH
CAR CO

CHAPTER THREE

The Newly Rich and the Industrial Titan

Cornelius Vanderbilt was the first true American titan. He was wealthy, powerful, and influential in forming the United States' identity. In many ways, Vanderbilt paved the road for business in American society and set the tone of big business for generations. He and the industrial titans that would follow him showed the power and control that big business would have and the incredible wealth made from massive industrial markets. With an estimated $100 million (over $2 billion in 2018) worth of assets at the time of his death, Vanderbilt was the richest man in America—until oil tycoon John D. Rockefeller stole the title.

Characterized by ingenuity, ruthless business sense, and undeniable wealth, the tycoons shaped the United

The Gilded Age was marked by the rising of titans of industry. The men depicted here (Vanderbilt is in first row, second person in) are all examples of the extremely wealthy class. Here they are testing out the subway construction in New York City.

John D. Rockefeller was the founder and head of the Standard Oil Company and the world's first billionaire.

and infamous.[3] Rockefeller began as a small-scale oil man in Cleveland, Ohio, dedicated to finding a way to turn his small refinery into a huge profit. America was enamored with light, and newly discovered kerosene was lighting the way to a very bright future. Unfortunately, refineries were rushing to put out enough oil to meet public demand, and improperly refined oil was not just incendiary; it was explosive. Rockefeller managed to revolutionize the way oil was refined so that the same standard quality of oil would always leave his refineries, and he could guarantee a certain level of safety through that process. He was unfailingly confident in his product and in himself.

Rockefeller set out to make his oil the standard by which all other oil was compared, and he succeeded. He boldly named his company the Standard Oil company, and he worked to make sure the product lived up to the name.

In the early days of Rockefeller's refinery, he partnered with Vanderbilt's railroads, promising that the rails would get exclusive rights to his oil in exchange for a low shipping price. Vanderbilt understood that oil was going to be a huge moneymaking venture and managed to partner with the right man in Rockefeller. Standard Oil was growing rapidly; its success was going to be unprecedented. The partnership was mutually beneficial and helped get Rockefeller's Standard Oil off the ground.

Vanderbilt and Rockefeller worked together for a time, but eventually Standard Oil outgrew the deal. Rockefeller turned to Vanderbilt's competitor, Thomas Scott. Rockefeller would move between the two railroaders for years, with each undercutting the other's prices to earn Standard Oil's business. After all, oil, especially Standard Oil, was good business to be in.

Rockefeller was an incredibly savvy businessman who began buying out other refineries early. With time, he created a monopoly on oil by buying out every other competitor and the markets surrounding production and processing of oil. The Standard Oil company was not just setting the standard anymore; it was the only real option.

Vanderbilt and Scott, both seeing the money that could be made, eventually tried to collaborate against Rockefeller to control the rate war that Rockefeller used against them. They tried to set a standard rate on the railroad for the shipping of oil by "price fixing" the market, a move that would be illegal in the future. By colluding to set a price, they were violating the concept of free market competition. The plan failed anyway. Instead, Rockefeller created the Standard Oil pipelines out of his refinery in Cleveland, Ohio, which carried oil to his markets. He had created the Standard Oil Trust by controlling the production, processing, transport, and sale of oil. It also made him filthy rich.

It would take the Sherman Antitrust Act of 1890 to finally stop Rockefeller and Standard Oil's control of the oil market, but before that could happen, Rockefeller amassed an obscene amount of money. He was the first billionaire in America, and even his philanthropic donations counted into the millions. According to *Forbes* magazine, when Rockefeller died in 1937, his "assets equaled 1.5 percent of America's total economic output."[4] He had a net worth of $10 billion ($340 billion in 2018).

Daniel Drew, Jay Gould, and Jim Fisk

Jay Gould, Daniel Drew, and Jim Fisk made up a band that would become one of Vanderbilt's greatest rivals late in life. Gould was a bold man who thrived off of financial disruption and became a leader among the railroad titans. Daniel Drew

THE GILDED AGE

The "Gilded Age" was a term coined by the writer Mark Twain about the era surrounding the Industrial Revolution and wealth that came from the captains of industry like Rockefeller and Carnegie. Originally the title of one of his novels, Twain's "gilded age" came to characterize the era and stood for the "graft, materialism, and corruption of public life" that came with industrialization.[5] Though Vanderbilt lived just prior to this time, embraced a more frugal lifestyle, and was not much of a philanthropist, he set the stage for men like Rockefeller and Carnegie. Vanderbilt's wealth also fed into the Gilded Age through his heir, William Vanderbilt. Essentially, the Gilded Age was characterized by mega wealth.

The term "gilded" pokes at the darkness that lay beneath the veneer of extreme wealth. Such excess and spending often came at the expense of exploited workers and unregulated businesses. People toiled in dangerous factories for incredibly low wages, while the titans and upper classes grew increasingly wealthier.

An excellent example of the opulent wealth displayed during this period can be seen on New York City's Fifth Avenue, also known as "Millionaire Row." Starting with the mansion of John Jacob Astor and including homes like the "Vanderbilt Triple Palace," built after the Commodore's death by his son William, one can see the ostentatious wealth of the newly rich that came with the industrial economy.

Meanwhile, the poor were stacked on top of each other in cramped and dangerous tenements. Today in contemporary society there remains a huge disparity in the distribution of wealth in America reminiscent of the industrial era and the Gilded Age.

ran the Erie Railway and was a cheat who worked with and against Vanderbilt's railroad interests throughout their dealings. Jim Fisk was known for his "bad business" and worked with Gould to disrupt the markets and profit off of financial panics that would ensue from them. The three were robber barons, a term coined to describe businessmen during the 1800s who used unethical and unfair business practices to become rich. They were also three of the biggest thorns in Vanderbilt's side while he built his railroad empire.

The three orchestrated one of Vanderbilt's largest failures during his professional career, the Erie Railway hostile takeover in 1867. A hostile takeover involves an outside party coming in and buying up a large portion of a company's stock in order to gain the controlling portion of stock. This gives the person the controlling interest in the company and essentially puts them in charge of the company.

Jay Gould, Daniel Drew, and Jim Fisk knew of Vanderbilt's desire for Daniel Drew's railway line. Drew had played Vanderbilt previously, in 1863, and had worked against Vanderbilt in secret, and Vanderbilt was out for revenge. He wanted to ruin Drew, and meant to do so through the Erie Railway. Vanderbilt began buying large portions of stock to take out Drew, but Drew, Fisk, and Gould had a plan. Gould used a loophole to print $10 million (over $160 million in 2018) of convertible bonds under the Erie Railway charter that he turned into stock (the move would eventually become illegal in the United States). Essentially, this made for hugely inflated stock—producing more of it to decrease the value of individual pieces. Vanderbilt spent huge sums of money on stock that was rendered nearly valueless. He could not buy enough to gain a controlling stock option because there was simply too much stock to buy.

When Vanderbilt discovered what had been done, he sought out legal support, and a judge issued warrants for the arrest of Gould, Drew, and Fisk, even though the Erie charter was written in a way that would have technically made the creation of the bonds legal. Regardless, the three men fled New York to New Jersey to avoid arrest. Eventually, Gould grew tired and returned to New York with a huge amount of money. He was arrested but paid his way off and returned to business, funded in part by the money Vanderbilt paid to buy the useless Erie Railway stock.

Thomas Scott and Andrew Carnegie

Thomas Scott was one of Cornelius Vanderbilt's competitors when he joined the railroad industry. Scott ran the Pennsylvania Railroad after moving up through the ranks of the company. Andrew Carnegie was his protégé. It was Scott who taught Carnegie the nuances of investment. It was also under Scott's skillful guidance that the Pennsylvania Railroad saw some of its greatest gains through smart business savvy, like cutting prices and laying new lines. He also had interests in the Texas and Pacific Railway and hoped to have a transcontinental railroad that never came to fruition.

Scott did blunder in his dealings with John D. Rockefeller. When the two partnered over the transport of Standard Oil, there were some disagreements between them, which led to Rockefeller shutting down refineries in Pittsburgh, Pennsylvania. With less oil to move, Scott chose to stop running some trains out of Pittsburgh to cut costs. This was not received well by the people who relied on the railroad for a livelihood and were laid off because of Scott's decision. A riot broke out in Pittsburgh in 1877. People died, and $5 million

Andrew Carnegie was a Scottish immigrant who made his fortune in steel toward the end of Vanderbilt's life. He was a great philanthropist.

(over $113 million in 2018) worth of property damage was done, with Pennsylvania Railroad feeling the impact of some of that damage. Other than that, Scott was successful and a good mentor to Andrew Carnegie.

Carnegie soaked up everything he could from Scott's strong business sense. Originally from Dunfermline, Scotland,

Carnegie came from a hardworking family that had fallen on difficult times. Starting off at Pennsylvania Railroad, Carnegie followed Scott's tutelage and saw some success with investments through Pennsylvania, but it was not where he would stay.

Carnegie ultimately made his fortune in steel once he left the railroad in 1865. Embracing the Bessemer steelmaking process, Carnegie managed to stay just ahead of the markets in the steel industry, buying up businesses relevant to steel production for years.

In 1889, Carnegie grouped his steel interests in the Carnegie Steel Company, which basically ran the steel market from then on. It was hugely successful, and he became very wealthy. In 1901, Carnegie sold Carnegie Steel to J.P. Morgan for $250 million (over $7 billion in 2018) and retired to pursue philanthropic interests.

New Money

Vanderbilt started a trend in society by creating the standard for the American businessman. He was a forerunner of the "new money" era that launched the industrial tycoons and created economic markets that allowed industrialists to become incredibly wealthy. His actions impacted global markets and American business for generations. Interactions with tycoons and fellow industrialists shaped the market that exists today and helped craft the American business identity. It was the actions of these tycoons that created an economic model of extreme wealth that transformed the United States into a wealthy nation and through that into a superpower.

Vanderbilt was the first tycoon.

CHAPTER FOUR

Tycoon

Cornelius Vanderbilt accomplished incredible feats and held two successful industrial empires in his lifetime. He claimed the shipping industry in his youth, running and controlling a large portion of the shipping out of New York City. He manipulated the market with ease and great success. In his more senior years, Vanderbilt recognized the changing market and ran full force into railroads. He constructed one of the largest and most successful railroad companies of the time.

With his sheer success, Vanderbilt was a force among men, respected and revered by competitors. More than anything, though, Vanderbilt helped shape the way business was done in the nineteenth century. By setting precedents in his shipping industry and later in railroads for business dealings and possessing a fiercely competitive nature that

Railroads became increasingly important in the second half of the nineteenth century. This image shows a train stopping in New York City in 1880.

rarely let him back down from a challenge, he was a serious competitor and tycoon. Titans would follow his example. Being as successful in one market as Vanderbilt was would have been impressive. To do it twice over was astounding.

The Dispatch Line

Cornelius Vanderbilt launched the Dispatch Line on the Hudson River shortly after he left the employ of the Union Line. Initially working with three boats, this was just the starting point of an eventual empire. He operated predominantly in the waters in and around New York at the beginning, gradually spreading out until he controlled most of the local shipping in and out of the state. He was ruthless as a competitor.

When a line got in his way, Vanderbilt would buy it out, or drop his rates so low that it would force the competitor to come to the table and buy Vanderbilt off. That became Vanderbilt's methodology—get what he wanted from a competitor by any legal means necessary. He was known to run a line against a competitor with single-minded dedication of forcing the competitor's hand. To do so, Vanderbilt would continuously and dramatically cut fares. In turn, the competitor would have to drop their fares. Vanderbilt would merely drop his prices again. A rate war would ensue, but few competitors were wealthy enough to truly compete with the Commodore. They would be forced out of business or forced into meeting with Vanderbilt to buy him off.

Though perhaps some competitors, especially those forced to the Commodore's will, would question his morals and his ethics, Vanderbilt lived by a careful code and worked hard to respect the deals he made. Competitors may not have always seen that, but it was important to Vanderbilt that he maintained an honorable reputation. Yes, he was ruthless and relentless, but he rarely broke a deal unless he believed someone else broke it first.

Moving South

In 1848, California struck gold. A mass pilgrimage followed and people flooded into the state looking to make it rich. Vanderbilt found his own way to get his cut of the money being made. He expanded his shipping industry to meet the needs of the American people.

At the time of the gold rush, for people outside of California, getting there could require a long journey. Covered wagons could be used to take the land route over plains and through mountain passes. The trip could take anywhere from three to seven months and transverse more than 3,000 miles (4,828 km). That said, travelers could also take the route around Cape Horn, the southern tip of South America, which would last anywhere from four to eight months on a ship, but the cost of the journey was expensive. Finally, people could take a theorized Panama Canal route that took two to three months, but risked exposure to hot climate diseases like malaria—and they had to dig the canal first. Vanderbilt saw another option. He was going to make a route through Nicaragua, and it was going to be faster than the other options.

Vanderbilt went so far as to draw plans with the Nicaraguan government to construct a canal creating an all-water route from the Caribbean to the Pacific. However, the canal was never built. Vanderbilt, though, did succeed in creating a route through the country, albeit using a combination of water and land. The route took a steamer from New York to the Caribbean port city of San Juan del Norte. From there,

THE HUDSON RIVER

One of the most valuable routes in American history is that of the Hudson River. One of the reasons the British took New York during the American Revolution was to control the Hudson. It gave the British army access to interior forts and allowed for easy trade with the motherland. After the revolution and industrialization, trade on the Hudson meant access to New York City. As a result of industrialization, New York continued to be an important port and quickly became a huge hub for business. Vanderbilt started and built an empire based on trade on the Hudson and movement in and out of New York from Staten Island.

As industrialization continued, New York only grew more important to the United States. Desire to run steamship lines on the Hudson fueled many of the rate wars that made Vanderbilt so successful. In many ways, travel on the Hudson meant making money for anyone willing to fight for it.

The Hudson River and New York City were hugely impactful on Vanderbilt's rise, providing the impetus for a great deal of his earliest success.

travelers would take the San Juan River to Lake Nicaragua and the city of Rivas, where a stagecoach would run to the Pacific port of San Juan del Sur. The final leg took a steamer from there to San Francisco, California, to strike Vanderbilt's version of gold—huge earning potential. The venture made Vanderbilt a very wealthy man through shipping, passengers, and noncompeting clauses.

Changing Times

Cornelius Vanderbilt amassed his fortune by embracing new technologies and new markets at just the right time. Railroads began gaining prominence in the 1830s but really gained popularity in the 1850s, and he was all aboard.

As Vanderbilt saw when steamships began overtaking traditional shipping on the Hudson, the times were changing again. New markets were taking over, and Vanderbilt began preparing for a new venture. While working on "the Southern Route" through Nicaragua, he began liquidating his northern shipping routes whenever the offered price was right. The business world was changing, railroads were rising, and tensions were mounting with the South.

At the start of the Civil War, Vanderbilt's net worth was near $20 million (over $538 million in 2018), and his business bided well through the war and even expanded yet again. In 1860, Vanderbilt acquired his first railroad, the Long Island Railroad, to connect with his ferry there. It offered an opportunity to draw his son William into the business and would be the start of his second empire. One year before the nation found peace in 1865, Vanderbilt retired from shipping with a net worth close to $30 million dollars (over $807 million in 2018).

A Second Empire

Vanderbilt's second enterprise, railroads, made him increasingly famous and infamous. Modern writers contest his role as a robber baron or a captain of industry. Others refer to him as a king. What is undeniable is that he was grossly successful within his market. The year 1864 marked his seventieth birthday and rather than slow down, Vanderbilt was running full steam ahead.

At the close of the Civil War, Vanderbilt saw a changing world. The American market, transport, and shipping industries were changing, and the nation's lands were being stitched together by railroads. Vanderbilt had made a huge fortune in shipping. He was one of the wealthiest people alive during the antebellum period and had survived the Civil War and came out richer for it. During the late 1850s and early 1860s, and using some of that massive wealth, Vanderbilt began exploring railroad options around New York.

One of his earliest buys was with the New York & Harlem Railroad. This transaction also showed how powerful Vanderbilt was. The previous president of the railroad, Robert Schuyler, had found himself in serious debt and on the verge of bankruptcy. Some of that debt was due to Vanderbilt. As railroads were increasingly important in the New York Stock Exchange, the failings of a large railroad like the New York & Harlem had potential to shake the market and cause stock prices to plummet. Vanderbilt, who was an active investor in the market, attempted to intervene to preserve his own interests. He granted a sizable loan to Schuyler and drove up stock options to stabilize the market. Schuyler swindled him.

In an effort to save himself, Schuyler printed $1.9 million (over $53 million in 2018) worth of illegal stock in the railroad.

The *Commodore Vanderbilt* was built by the American Locomotive Company to run on the Hudson River Railway, another important railroad among Vanderbilt's many holdings.

All he ended up doing was committing fraud, and he made the market plummet. He also put Vanderbilt, now a primary shareholder, in a huge bind. Share values plummeted. As biographer T.J. Stiles puts it, "The man scorned as 'boorish' by New York's elite had done his best to save the most elite of them all, and had been repaid with treachery."[1] Some of the shares Vanderbilt had purchased were falsely printed stock, but some were legitimate. However, the railroad, which had been hit hard financially in the wake of Schuyler's betrayal, refused to pay dividends on Vanderbilt's stock, including the legitimate stock. Vanderbilt was furious. In response, he won himself a seat on the board to wrest a portion of the control of the railroad. He

served alongside his son-in-law and Daniel Drew. From there he manipulated his role until he had a controlling and vested interest in the railroad.

Vanderbilt was also excellent at manipulating the market to his advantage. For example, Daniel Drew was up to his old tricks in 1863. He saw an opportunity to drive up the stock prices with a quick and heavy buy, then sell it just as quickly. By doing so, he would cause the stock value to plummet with a large sell out. Drew stood to make a lot of money, but investors not privy to the deal stood to lose even more. Unfortunately for those other investors, the plummeting value would ruin their stock options.

Vanderbilt learned of the plan and bought massive amounts of stock when the opportunity presented itself, driving prices up incredibly high. When the stock plummeted, many of the investors took losses, Drew among them. Vanderbilt, however, came out richer and owning the controlling stock of the New York & Harlem Railroad.

Using his new power, he placed William as the vice president and established the Vanderbilt name firmly in railroads. More than anything, the New York & Harlem acquisition showed the men on Wall Street that though the industry had changed, Vanderbilt was still the same. He was rich, he was shrewd, and he was not afraid of competition.

Railroad King

Working in railroads was somewhat different for Vanderbilt than working in the shipping market. While shipping was competitive, railroads were vicious. Players like Drew, Gould, and Fisk abounded, and a player on the field had to be good with the stock market. While shipping lines were owned outright, railroads were invested. Companies were divided into stock options, which wealthy investors would purchase. The number of shares a person owned bought them voting seats on the boards that controlled the interests of the railroad. The more stock a person had, the more control the person had over the railroad and the more money said person stood to make from it.

One of the most important investments for Vanderbilt was through his earliest railroad acquisition. Being named director of the New York & Harlem Railroad also gave him access to one of the most significant pieces of infrastructure to date, a railroad bridge across the Hudson River near Albany, New

York. By spanning the Hudson, the bridge allowed trains from New York City—now a huge shipping city and one of the most valuable ports—to connect with the rest of the country. The bridge was thus pivotal in trade and travel into and out of New York, and by controlling the New York & Harlem Railroad, Vanderbilt also controlled the bridge. He used that power viciously.

In 1866, Vanderbilt's railroads were competing with the New York Central Railroad. He had initially sent his son William to arbitrate and find a resolution, but the efforts failed, with the representatives allegedly not taking the Commodore seriously. They would rue the day.

When the competitors failed to meet with Vanderbilt and William in New York on a set meeting date, Vanderbilt closed his bridge to the opposing railroad. The New York Central no longer had a route into or out of New York City. New York Central's business was decimated. The competitors scrambled to meet with Vanderbilt to resolve the issue. Vanderbilt chose to play his cards, instead letting the opposing railroad slowly choke into submission. It was acts like this that contributed to Vanderbilt's brute-like and robber baron image.

New York Central passengers were forced to find other means into the city. The conflict ended in the courts, and Vanderbilt was faced with the question of why he had not initially taken the legal route to solve the problem, as he had grounds to do so. His response was, "It is not according to my mode of doing things, to bring suit against a man that I have the power in my own hands to punish … The law, as I view it, goes too slow for me when I have the remedy in my own hands. Let the other parties go to the law if they want, but by God I think I know what the law is; I have had enough of it."[2] Vanderbilt knew the value of the law. He had mentored under

Thomas Gibbons, an accomplished lawyer, who had impacted the control of state regulation on trade with *Gibbons v. Ogden*. It was not that Vanderbilt did not respect the law; it was that he was relentless and efficient. He wanted the quickest result, and his methods worked.

The New York Central Railroad came to the negotiating table within days of the blockade, and Vanderbilt came out the victor. New York Central agreed to keep freight running in and out of the city rather than in one direction, to pay a portion of the Hudson Railroad's terminal charges, and make a payment of $100,000 (over $2.6 million in 2018) in concessions to end the blockade. More than that, the blockade broke the spirit of board members of the competing railroad, and they sold their stock. Vanderbilt and his associates bought the stock cheap.

In 1867, Cornelius Vanderbilt was named president of the New York Central. Vanderbilt was dubbed the railroad king by the media, and effectively held control over one of the most powerful rail routes in the United States, as well as the routes that connected that line to New York City. The New York Central Railroad would become his link, making for one of the longest rail lines to date. He was building a new empire by using the tools that had made him successful initially. His lines consolidated into the first real corporation.

The American Railroad

Over the coming years, Vanderbilt would acquire several other railroads. Rather than build new lines like some of his competitors, Vanderbilt would invest in and buy already established railroads, connecting his acquisitions into his line. In some cases, such as with the Hudson, he would buy when they were struggling and revitalize them. Eventually,

Vanderbilt would own vested interests in the Hudson River Railroad, the Central Railroad, and the Long Island Railroad. These interests would be consolidated into the New York Central Railroad.

From there, Vanderbilt spread west. He bought into the Lakeshore & Michigan Railway, the Michigan Southern, the Canadian Southern, and the Michigan Central Railroad, which gave him access all the way to Chicago, Illinois, and St. Louis, Missouri. It was a huge railroad empire marked by double-tracked rails that allowed trains to come and go concurrently.

Within five years of starting in railroads, Vanderbilt made approximately $25 million (over $491 million in 2018). Vanderbilt's train empire grew fast and made money equally quickly. Business was booming. In total, Vanderbilt's lines were more effective and successful. They were known to be safe, as "twenty-six deaths and seventy-two injuries resulted from accidents on the Erie, but all of Vanderbilt's railroads put together registered a total of only eleven injuries—no fatalities at all."[3] By 1876, Vanderbilt was running an incredibly fast train between Chicago and New York. A rider could be in Chicago in a mere twenty-six hours. An effective businessman, Vanderbilt is remembered for how "he bought up stock in local railroads, ultimately combining them into a vast transportation network and a powerful family empire that transformed New York's infrastructure and reshaped the region."[4]

The Grand Central Depot

The Grand Central Depot broke ground in 1869. Opened on Forty-Second Street as the New York City train hub for the Hudson Railroad, the New Haven Railroad, and the

Grand Central Depot was Vanderbilt's final huge project. Today, it is known as Grand Central Terminal.

NEW-YORK & HARLEM R.R.

Harlem Railroad, Grand Central was a huge undertaking. The construction took three years to complete and $6.5 million (over $114 million in 2018) to finance. It contained different sections, one per railroad. The first trains pulled into the depot in 1871, and it was not long before *Railway Age* magazine reported "170 trains a day at Grand Central."[5]

The station was huge and busy, and not completely well received. The large number of tracks were dangerous and earned Vanderbilt quite a bit of criticism. That many trains running all day long made a great deal of smoke and pollution. Furthermore, the tracks were dangerous in uncovered high-traffic areas, which led to protests. Vanderbilt offered limited options to solve the problem. He only became truly motivated when the public learned of an initial agreement that had been made prior to constructing the depot. It stated that the rail lines would be shut down if they disrupted the normal use of the streets. Faced with the possibility of closing lines, Vanderbilt spent an additional $6 million (over $131 million in 2018) in 1875 to create iron bridges to allow for public traffic to cross the tracks.

Not surprisingly, due to the ever-increasing popularity of trains, shortly after Vanderbilt died, the station could not keep up with the traffic that ran through it. It would undergo multiple renovations and alterations until it would become what it is today, Grand Central Terminal.

Vanderbilt

Vanderbilt was uniquely positioned in time and space to be hugely successful, but his skills and personality enabled him to accomplish all that he did. Brash, forceful, and incredibly hardworking, Vanderbilt was frugal and diligent, which enabled him to churn money back into his businesses early on and invest widely much later. He was arrogant, making claims like, "Let them do what I have done."[6] But that confidence served him well. Though he had very little formal education, he was incredibly smart and dedicated to learning his chosen professions. He was a perfect example of a businessman who could recognize the next big thing and find a way to profit off it. There is a reason that at the time of his death, Vanderbilt was one of the wealthiest men in America: he was single-minded in his pursuit of success.

CHAPTER FIVE

Industrialism and the Free Market

Cornelius Vanderbilt was, in many ways, a man of his time. He had a roughneck, hardworking blue-collar quality, but came to dominate the business world—a true self-made man. In fact, it was success stories like Vanderbilt's that sold the idea of the American dream—the notion that hard work can pay off tenfold. That said, there is no ignoring the fact that part of Vanderbilt's great success hinged on the era he was born into. Nineteenth-century America was a breeding ground for incredible success stories. New industrial markets were created often, and the thirst for technology created a vortex where tycoons like Vanderbilt could flourish. Part

Cornelius Vanderbilt became a titan of his own time and remains a famous name today. This statue sits on Vanderbilt University's campus.

of the success of men like Vanderbilt was directly indicative of the changing society in which they existed. The identity of the era was one of growth and progress. For a man like Vanderbilt, such a setting was the perfect place to flourish.

Manifest Destiny

"Manifest destiny," a term coined in 1845 by journalist John Louis O'Sullivan, is an excellent example of the American mindset during the nineteenth century. O'Sullivan lambasted

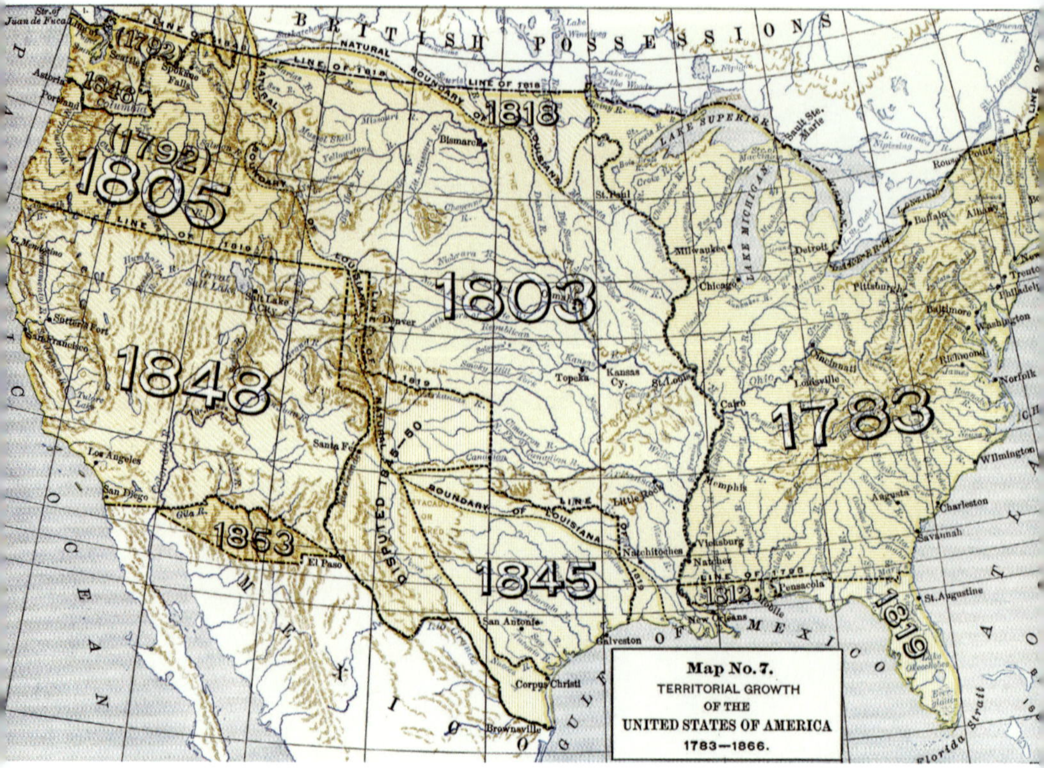

This map depicts land acquisitions, and the year the land was acquired, as manifest destiny gradually expanded the United States' boundary westward.

those who stood in the way of the United States' "fulfillment of our manifest destiny to overspread the continent."[1] It hinged on extreme nationalism and patriotic support. The idea was that the United States was destined to span from ocean to ocean. Some people believed it was a divine right, granted by God to the American people. In other instances, heading west just seemed like the thing to do. It was an overarching optimism that American growth was destined. The patriots had won the revolution and the Americans had won the War of 1812. Now the next land for them to conquer was that which spanned toward California.

There is an arrogant confidence to the idea of manifest destiny, but it was one that came to fruition. Many in the nation believed that it should span from coast to coast, and so it did. That sort of arrogance that the nation was destined to be large and powerful fueled the people and the growth of the country. There was a spirit in the air during the 1800s that built on that optimistic arrogance. Industrialization and expansion created wealth and power. For someone like Vanderbilt, that was an environment where his bold confidence and skills were needed. Both the country and business worlds were growing rapidly with few restraints and constraints. Empires were possible and, in some ways, inevitable.

Laissez-Faire in the Air

Early in American history, businesses and markets were given mostly free rein. The economy was built on a laissez-faire model that fit with the spirit of the age. Part of the foundation of American society was a rebellious nature that would persist for generations that coincided with the laissez-faire model.

Later, in the nineteenth century, America was laissez-faire when it came to business. A French word meaning "to let do" or "leave alone," laissez-faire business meant that the government mostly stayed out of business interests. The federal government did have controlling interests over the nation, but the states, for the most part, regulated their business interests. When Vanderbilt entered the market as a young man, that was still true. America was well on its way to a capitalist system with a free market economy.

The Capitalist

The American laissez-faire mentality encouraged capitalism in the United States. Capitalism is an economy and/or government where trade and industry are held by private parties instead of being vested in the state. Business interests and decisions are made by private owners with financial interest in the companies that supply goods or services to the public rather than by the government. A capitalist is a person who invests in economic capitalism. Essentially, the people who own businesses in a capitalist economy are the ones making decisions about the markets and products available. This creates a free market.

A free market is where the price of a good or service is named by the businesses that supply them. There is competition in a free market because multiple businesses compete for the money of the people who are buying the good or the service. For example, the rate wars that Vanderbilt was legendary for were a product of a free market, capitalist system. Vanderbilt and his competitors set the prices on their fares for their ferries and trains to compete for passenger support. Vanderbilt would drop the cost of his fares in order to try to attract people to his ferry line. Competitors would drop their fares to compete

This engraving of Cornelius Vanderbilt was created by George Edward Perine around 1860.

with Vanderbilt's price or risked losing their passengers to Vanderbilt's cheaper fares.

Ultimately, Vanderbilt was very much a capitalist. He often invested in other people's businesses to make money, and he used the free market to his advantage, as shown with the fare wars and railroads. More than anything, the Industrial Revolution and the incredible wealth earned by industrial tycoons was a direct result of the free market system in the United States. Competition enabled the tycoons to beat out competitors and grow wealthier. That said, an unchecked system came with its faults and struggles. In the case of the unchecked free market of the early nineteenth-century economy, one of the biggest issues was the monopoly.

Monopolies

A monopoly is when one person or business sells a product or service without any competitors. In the case of Robert Livingston's and Robert Fulton's monopoly on ferry traffic on the Hudson in the nineteenth century, that was a legal monopoly granted by New York State to Livingston. It essentially said that Livingston and Fulton had the exclusive right to control the use of steamships on the Hudson River for trade. That meant a person could not run a steamship on the Hudson without Livingston's and Fulton's approval. Though Vanderbilt was offered work through Livingston, he chose to fight the monopoly and continue to work with Gibbons. Vanderbilt was quoted as saying, "I don't care half so much about making money as I do about making my point, and coming out ahead."[2] Vanderbilt believed deeply in the free market system.

When Thomas Gibbons took *Gibbons v. Ogden* to the Supreme Court, he was also pitting some of the newly created

Robert Fulton revolutionized the transport industry with his ships and changed American trade and business forever.

federal power in the Constitution against state power. By ruling the way it did, the Supreme Court took a stance on state power verses federal power, and vested the power of interstate trade in the hands of the federal government. The *Gibbons v. Ogden* ruling maintained the free market and the right to compete on the Hudson River and made the decree that states could not set laws that limited interstate commerce or trade.

Essentially, the battle fought by Gibbons and Vanderbilt against Livingston and Fulton changed national business regulations and limited states' rights over controlling some of the trade in and out of their states. It was an important court case that has affected trade within the United States ever since.

Government and Business

The industrialists, including Vanderbilt, needed the free market system because their success was rooted in competition. That said, a totally unregulated market came with risks. People did business to suit their own needs. They could create and destroy markets, for the good of their own wallet, even at the detriment of the whole nation. The industrial market was fiercely competitive and not for the faint of heart.

Vanderbilt fit well among the ranks. The Commodore was not afraid to use any tool in his arsenal in the game of competition. He understood the value of the courts, as shown with the way he and Gibbons handled the Livingston monopoly, but he could compete as a businessman as well. There is a story that at one point, when Vanderbilt realized that two business allies had betrayed him, he wrote a letter that said, "You have undertaken to cheat me. I won't sue you, for the law is too slow. I'll ruin you."[3] That was the Vanderbilt way. In a capitalist system, such revenge was possible.

However, an unchecked system can have side effects. Capitalism can create systems where the rich get richer and the poor get poorer if there is no one to protect the interests of the consumers and regulate the market. In the case of the Industrial Revolution, many of the victims took the form of the poor and working classes. The American response was sure to come, and it came in the form of the Progressive Era, but not until after Vanderbilt's death. He was a man in a barely regulated free market who used competition and capitalism to make himself insanely rich. He was the epitome of the American businessman during the nineteenth century.

Vanderbilt the Industrialist

Vanderbilt was singular in his success. According to history writer Robert McNamara, "Vanderbilt's control of the American transportation business was so extensive that anyone wishing to travel or ship goods had no choice but to contribute to his growing fortune."[4] Though others would come after him and see even greater wealth and prosperity in the American market, he was the first to tackle that market and manipulate it for his ever-increasing success. He was the first industrialist to not only take on two independent, brand-new markets but also dominate those markets. His southern shipping route and railroads fed the manifest destiny mentality and connected the Northeast to the Midwest unlike ever before. It was his brilliance and efforts that helped make the steamship market and feed the railroad market to create a prosperous future that would help define America as a country. American business was partially shaped by Cornelius Vanderbilt.

It has to be acknowledged that part of Vanderbilt's success was determined by fate. The Commodore was born into a

No businessman had quite the impact on the American economy like Vanderbilt had. Here he is depicted in the late 1870s.

shipping family at the start of the industrial era, in New York, which would become the heart of business. The stars aligned to grant him a unique opportunity. He was born in an era that suited his unique talents.

Something about Vanderbilt was specifically well suited to the market and environment of the nineteenth century. It is because of this that Vanderbilt's triumphs must be credited to him exclusively. Vanderbilt was born for a capitalist system. He was bold and ruthless and brilliant. Competition should have been his middle name. The way he did business helped establish and entrench the American economy into a free market capitalist system, which would be emulated by future businessmen. In fact, Vanderbilt, through *Gibbons v. Ogden*, was an impetus of the capitalist, free market trade system that would flourish on the Hudson River and help turn New York into the industrial metropolis it would become in the 1900s.

His capitalist mentality and methodologies would help define business for the nineteenth century and, through that, the United States' identity as a nation. Vanderbilt survived industrialization, the Civil War, and saw the beginning of Reconstruction, and he made a fortune while doing it. He created a reputable and reliable rail service that was one of the leading industries in the nation.

Vanderbilt had controlling interests in rails that connected the Midwest to the East Coast in an unprecedented manner. His efforts stitched the jumbled and disordered railways of New York into a comprehensive system that unified the country like never before. He had the pulse of New York under his thumb and controlled the rail market confidently and comfortably.

During his life, Vanderbilt helped change trade laws with shipping, defined unprecedented routes with railroads, and in turn helped chauffer New York City into its role as an American business hub.

There is little doubt that Cornelius Vanderbilt defined his time and his era. He was the first captain of industry and a forerunner in American ideology. The Commodore helped shape his country.

CHAPTER SIX

Legacy

Today, modern America is vastly different and yet almost entirely the same as the America that Cornelius Vanderbilt helped create. The economy still reflects the influence of industrialists and capitalists like Vanderbilt and the other industrial titans, but the industrial titan has been replaced with the Silicon Valley developer and the social media mogul. The titles are different and the mediums they trade in have evolved dramatically, but competition still reigns supreme. The impact of the Industrial Revolution and the wealthy men who led the industrialization of the United States of America can still be felt today. Vanderbilt and his

Vanderbilt's legacy lived on in his children, grandchildren, and great-grandchildren, as well as in his reputation. Here, grandchildren Cornelius and Gladys pose for a picture around 1900.

compatriots helped shape the last 150 years of American history with their tycoon business practices and ruthless capitalist markets. As the first industrial titan, Cornelius Vanderbilt helped forge the nation out of steam power and railroad ties. Vanderbilt did not just run a shipping company and control one of the largest railroads of his time. He helped fuel a changing American economy, and through that, he helped create a nation.

Civil War and Reconstruction

Vanderbilt was one of the few titans who saw the beginnings of the industrial era in America. Some of the first influential and successful industrial markets in America were textiles and steamships. Though textile manufacturing came before Vanderbilt, he was at the heart of steamships. He also witnessed a large majority of the nineteenth century and survived as a businessman through most of it.

Vanderbilt witnessed his nation industrialize, and helped form American capitalism. He also helped set the ruthless tone of American business within that industrialization. The titans who would rise in his wake would help perfect that model, and it would carry the country into the future.

Even more than that, however, Vanderbilt helped the nation through some of its darkest times. The donation of the *Vanderbilt* steamship during the Civil War gave the Union a desperately needed edge on the waters. After the Civil War, the United States had to be rebuilt, and the Reconstruction era began. In 1873, the donation Vanderbilt extended to a Southern university helped establish some goodwill between two badly beaten sides of a ravaged country. It was during the time of Reconstruction that the industrial titans would truly rise, and the Vanderbilt legacy would begin to shine.

Due to the natures of their businesses, many industrialists became quite wealthy during and after the Civil War. While the rest of the nation floundered to reconstruct a destroyed country, the industrialists had provided the fuel and the tools of the war and so came out wealthier. Though Vanderbilt had not intended to directly profit off of war, trade during wartime was a profitable business. Others fared well too. Once the war was over, industrialists continued to succeed, and they had the Vanderbilt example to learn from.

Industrialists like John D. Rockefeller and Andrew Carnegie were cutthroat capitalists who dominated their chosen markets much like Vanderbilt had. They used similar tools like rate wars and takeovers to create monopolies in their chosen fields. Rockefeller's Standard Oil flourished in the years following Reconstruction and would eventually become one of the most profitable trusts in American history. Carnegie Steel Company would be a leader within its market because of its massive size and incredible profits. Just as Vanderbilt had before them, they both would impact American business and business law.

The Progressive Era

Gibbons v. Ogden had set a precedent for federal involvement in national trade, but there were other issues from industrialization that needed to be handled. The following decades would be marked by social and political responses to the industrialization that Vanderbilt and the subsequent tycoons so gleefully created. The Progressive Era was the public response to the incredible power of the industrial titans and corrupt politicians who would come into power during and after Reconstruction. Such criticism was not uncommon, and with the incredible disregard for human safety and well being that accompanied the industrial model, it is no surprise that workers rose up in response.

Often hit with rancor for his business practices and because he was so publicly wealthy and popularized, Vanderbilt was a target for the media. Even the famous author Mark Twain took pot shots at Vanderbilt, going so far as to write an open letter to the Commodore shaming him and criticizing him for his failures in philanthropy prior to Vanderbilt's donation to what would become Vanderbilt University. Twain brutally claimed things against Vanderbilt supporters like, "You seem to be the idol of only a crawling swarm of small souls, who love to glorify your most flagrant unworthiness; or sing of your unimportant private habits and sayings and doings, as if your millions gave them dignity."[1]

Journalists and writers were some of the most influential people during the Progressive Era. Referred to as muckrakers, some journalists also exposed the darker sides of industrialization and pushed for social consciousness in business.

The media was a fuel for change and would directly impact government policy when it came to big business. The progressive ideas would also embed themselves in politics. Voters came out to the polls seeking change, and they found it with the twenty-sixth president of the United States, Theodore Roosevelt. The progressive president broke up trusts under the Sherman Antitrust Act and passed heavy legislation shaped around social justice. It was a marked step toward social change and political involvement in business.

Moving Toward the Modern Era

The years following the Progressive Era would continue to be marked by a metaphorical industrial stamp. The money made during industrialization and the stock market that would grow so strong during it would shape the United States into an important player in global politics. Some rebellious spirit would remain a constant in driving the continuation of a capitalist market. Money was and is power, and with such a strong economy, the United States would remain incredibly powerful for years to come. As a nation, America managed to rebuild after events including two World Wars, the Great Depression, and the Cold War. Fear of communism and socialism would fuel one of the tensest periods of US history during that era. So closely were Americans tied to capitalism and the free trade markets with their democracy that the second half of the twentieth century would be spent maintaining capitalist markets and democracies around the world during the Cold War era. The Industrial Revolution and industrialists like Vanderbilt had forged a strong and rich nation that would weather more than a century and a half of dramatic changes, in part due to the economy that they fed with their businesses.

Capitalism Today

Capitalism reigns supreme in America today, though a modern push toward equality and labor laws has led to far more government involvement in modern business. Vanderbilt's presence is still felt today too. Historical writer Robert McNamara explains his continued impact, saying, "His sprawling businesses were essentially prototypes of modern corporations."[2] The nation still runs on a free market, and competition still fuels the fire of business. Big business is still big business. Even more than that, ingenuity still drives the American market and, in many ways, the national identity. The industrial titan has paved the way for modern industry.

The end of the twentieth century saw yet another shift in business. The invention of computers, such as this very early computer (ENIAC), signaled an important shift in knowledge. The digital age was beginning and marked the start of the era of the new tycoon.

MODERN TYCOONS

Social media and technology tycoons like Mark Zuckerberg, the cofounder and CEO of social media site Facebook, and Bill Gates, Microsoft Corporation's founder and CEO, are just two examples of powerful people who are impacting society with their products. Zuckerberg has access to his consumers in a way that Vanderbilt never had. His whole company is designed around connecting people. While Vanderbilt relied on low fares to draw in customers, Zuckerberg does not even charge for use of his site. This is the power of the modern tycoon. Zuckerburg's net worth as of 2018 was $64.1 billion. Gates, with a net worth of $90.5 billion, is a philanthropist who made his money leading the technology market and providing a tool that humankind would struggle to live without, computers.

In the twenty-first century, controlling access to information and the tools that grant access to information is an incredibly big business. However, the trends in media switch far faster than the trends did for Vanderbilt. Apps and technology go out of date or cannot draw younger audiences, a problem that tech moguls, social media, and similar companies face today. There is always a new idea just around the corner. Every day, product developers foray into the digital market in hopes of snagging some of the incredible fortunes programmers and developers are garnering. The digital landscape is limitless, and the contemporary era would find it nearly impossible to survive without the digital tools that were not commonplace even thirty years ago.

Since the beginning of the Industrial Revolution until the present time, technology has driven society. New ideas and concepts create new markets. The modern digital age parallels the industrial age surprisingly well. Tools like computers and the internet have evolved rapidly and changed lives irrevocably, much like steam power and the railroad did during Vanderbilt's lifetime. From the internet's earliest prototypes in the 1960s to the spread of personal computers in the 1980s to new computer technologies being developed and presented today, the world has changed dramatically.

Locally and internationally, people are more connected than generations prior could have ever fathomed. In the same way railroads drew together the United States as a nation during the second half of the nineteenth century, computers and the internet connect the world today. They also represent the platform for the contemporary tycoon.

Silicon Valley and the Digital Tycoon

San Francisco and the Bay Area in California is to the modern tycoon what New York and Staten Island were to Cornelius Vanderbilt. Their empires, however, are much smaller—so small even that they fit in the palm of your hand. Companies like Apple produce technology that computes at an incredible rate of speed in cell phones that double as mini computers. Google provides information at rates and in quantities that boggle the mind. The digital era is dealing in information, the ability to access that information, and the digital technology that makes both of those things possible and available. These are the new tycoons, and they are just as powerful, or maybe even more so, than Vanderbilt and his contemporaries.

The industry of it, however, has not changed much. Competition is fierce, and new ethical debates are rising in the face of the ever-increasing streams of information that technological devices can deliver. One defining difference in recent years may be the relationship the modern tycoons have with politics. Where once politics was the tool used to curb the unjust business practices of industrial titans, such as with the trust busters of the Progressive Era and efforts of President Theodore Roosevelt, now the digital titans have become the ones curbing the politicians. The impact of social media on modern politics is unprecedented. Sites like Facebook and Twitter have become platforms for political campaigns, and candidates have lost campaigns because of social media efforts.

The power modern technology has given to modern digital tycoons is being likened to that of the industrial titans and Gilded Age tycoons, and the wage discrepancies continue. As Vanderbilt biographer T.J. Styles puts it, "Our lives are channeled once again through fewer and fewer companies controlled by a few men."[3]

Modern monopolies are technological monopolies. A few select companies dominate the technological markets. Just think of Apple, Microsoft, and Google. Their competitors are few and far between. There is great power in those organizations as well, especially because there is great wealth in them. Just as in Vanderbilt's era, what those moguls choose to do with their power could very well define the future of the United States.

Vanderbilt's Legacy

Commodore Cornelius Vanderbilt's legacy is not as discernable on the map of the United States as it is on the ideology of the United States. The days of big business in railroads have mostly passed, although rail companies and commuter lines do still exist. The same can be said of steam power and shipping industries. Today, air and automotive travel are the transportation preferences for many in the modern world. Regardless, Vanderbilt's influence remains.

A nation driven by big business, America can credit such big business presence today to Vanderbilt as well as the men who would follow him. As a shipping and railroad titan, Vanderbilt managed to connect the United States in ways previously not done. His ruthless manner and iron will formed two powerful businesses that in turn fortified the United States and fueled the Industrial Revolution. He was brash, hardworking, and competitive. While he struggled to be accepted in high society in the social world, he was incredibly respected in the business realm and was not afraid of a challenge. Both a patriot and a capitalist, Vanderbilt truly was an American businessman. Though not known for his philanthropy, he made one great contribution to what would eventually become Vanderbilt University. This act would help make strides in reunifying the Union. However, more than anything else, Cornelius Vanderbilt was very good at one thing: making money.

The industrial titans are often credited with forging America into a strong nation during its infancy, but Vanderbilt set the tone and the stage for the Gilded Age and the era of the titan. He was a man both of and before his time. Vanderbilt's willingness to seek new markets and embrace new concepts helped the economy form. When it came to shipping, he was among the first to use steam. He consolidated disjointed and less effective railroads. Even more than that, he embraced the conceptual economy of securities and bonds. Cornelius Vanderbilt was able to "[grasp] one of the great changes of American culture [during the nineteenth century]: the

Today, San Jose, California, is the heart and hub of Silicon Valley, itself the heart and hub of the technological and digital world. Many modern technological tycoons who control large parts of today's digital markets and economy are based here.

abstraction of economic reality," and he did it in such a way that the country would never be the same again.[4] His model of strict competition and ruthless methods defined the Gilded Age in a way that would shape American business forever. Rich and powerful men would come and go through the following generations, but only Commodore Cornelius Vanderbilt was the first true American tycoon.

CHRONOLOGY

1712 Thomas Newcomen patents the first steam-powered engine.

1765 The Watt steam engine is invented.

1789 Samuel Slater brings the Industrial Revolution to America with the water-powered textile mill.

1792 New York Stock Exchange opens under the name Buttonwood Agreement.

1794 Cornelius "the Commodore" Vanderbilt is born.

1805 Vanderbilt drops out of school and begins working in his father's ferry business.

1810 Vanderbilt buys his first periauger.

1813 Vanderbilt marries Sophia Johnson, his cousin.

1818 Vanderbilt goes to work for Thomas Gibbons on his steamer, *Mouse*, and builds the *Bellona*.

1824 *Gibbons v. Ogden* is decided by the Supreme Court.

1828 Vanderbilt leaves Gibbons's Union Line and commissions his first ship, the *Citizen*, acquires the *Emerald* and the *Bellona*, and launches his Dispatch Line.

1848 The California gold rush begins.

1853 Vanderbilt is approved to run a route by land over Nicaragua to create a shorter route from New York to California. The Vanderbilt family also takes a tour of Europe.

1856 Vanderbilt acquires stock interest in the Delaware, Lackawanna, & Western Railroad.

1857 Vanderbilt becomes director of New York & Harlem Railroad.

1860 Vanderbilt buys and completes the Staten Island Railroad.

1862 Vanderbilt donates the *Vanderbilt* to the Union army.

1863 Vanderbilt takes the controlling interest of the Harlem Railroad.

1864 Vanderbilt is awarded the Congressional gold medal by the government for his donation of the *Vanderbilt*. He also retires from shipping.

1866 Vanderbilt closes his Hudson River rail bridge to trains from rival companies.

1867 Vanderbilt is named president of New York Central Railroad. Gould, Drew, and Fisk foil Vanderbilt's takeover of Erie Railway.

1868 Sophia Vanderbilt dies.

1869 Vanderbilt marries his second wife, cousin Frank Armstrong Crawford.

1871 Grand Central Depot opens.

1873 Vanderbilt endows the Central University of Tennessee with a $1 million donation.

1877 Cornelius Vanderbilt dies at the age of eighty-two.

GLOSSARY

asylum A hospital for the mentally insane or disabled.

capitalism A type of economy or a political system where private investors set the prices of goods and services instead of the government.

Civil War A conflict lasting from 1861 to 1865 in the United States, where the South seceded from the North.

commodore A shipping captain or naval officer.

competitor A business rival or opposing company.

Confederacy The name for the group of Southern states that united after seceding from the Union during the Civil War.

economy The markets, wealth, and resources of a country.

fare The rate paid for passage on a ship or train.

free market An economy that is unrestricted by government and allows for competition between privately owned companies.

Gilded Age A period during the eighteenth century marked by wealth earned from the industrial age that was funded by unethical or unsavory business practices.

Grand Central Depot A large train station built by Cornelius Vanderbilt in Manhattan that would become Grand Central Terminal.

industrialization The mechanical and technological development of a country.

industry The market for the creation and sale of a good or service.

laissez-faire A hands-off approach to business where the government does not regulate markets or trade.

manifest destiny The belief that it was the United States' fate to span from East Coast to West Coast.

manufacturing The creation of goods using technologies, especially machines.

market A form or location for trade.

mogul A socially powerful person.

monopoly The exclusive control over an industry.

muckraker A journalist during the end of the eighteenth and early nineteenth centuries who exposed unjust business practices and criticized unethical business owners.

periauger A shallow sailing boat with two sails.

philanthropy The giving of money and resources to charity.

poor class A low-ranked section of society that make low or no wages.

railroad Parallel tracks that trains run on; also refers to the type of company that owns the trains running on the tracks.

rate war The continuous lowering of fares by two or more competitors in a free market.

robber baron An unethical businessman who profited off the losses of others during the Industrial Revolution.

securities Stocks or bonds that can be liquidated into cash.

shipping To transport goods by water.

Silicon Valley A nickname referring to part of the San Francisco Bay Area; made popular for the technology tycoons that have congregated there and set up headquarters.

steamboat A ship powered by a steam engine.

steam engine The first engine that used atmospheric pressure to power pistons to create energy.

stock exchange A market for the buying and selling of stocks or bonds.

titan In Vanderbilt's time, a wealthy businessman who controlled an industry.

trust Owning a monopoly on every aspect of an industry.

tycoon A rich and successful businessperson.

working class A sect of society employed for a wage doing manual or industrial labor.

SOURCES

CHAPTER ONE

1. "Thomas Newcomen," *BBC*, 2014, http://www.bbc.co.uk/history/historic_figures/newcomen_thomas.shtml.

2. Henry Petroski, "Engineering Harnessing Steam," *American Scientist*, Vol. 84, No. 1 (January–February 1996).

3. Gene Dattle, *Cotton and Race in the Making of American: The Human Costs of Economic Power* (Lanham, MD: Rowman & Littlefield Publishing Group, Inc., 2009), xi.

4. Peter G. Goheen, "Industrialization and the Growth of Cities in the Nineteenth-Century America," *American Studies*, Vol. 14, No. 1 (spring 1973).

5. Paul H. Cootner, "The Role of Railroads in the United States Economic Growth," *The Journal of Economic History*, Vol. 23, No. 4 (December 1963).

CHAPTER TWO

1. T.J. Stiles, interviewed by Steve Inskeep, "Pugilistic Tycoon: Vanderbilt Jabs His Way To The Top," *NPR*, December 29, 2009, https://www.npr.org/templates/story/story.php?storyId=121998616.

2. Dorothy Kelly MacDowell, "From the Book *Commodore Vanderbilt and His Family,*" Long Island Genealogy, http://longislandgenealogy.com/Surname_Pages/vanderbilt.htm.

3. Edward J. Renehand Jr., *Commodore: the Life of Cornelius Vanderbilt* (New York: Basic Books, 2007), 113.

4. T.J. Stiles, *The Frist Tycoon: The Epic Life of Cornelius Vanderbilt* (New York: Vintage, 2009), 565.

5. Light, Larry, "What Cornelius Vanderbilt Can Teach Investors Today," *Forbes*, March 29, 2016, https://www.forbes.com/sites/lawrencelight/2016/03/29/what-cornelius-vanderbilt-can-teach-investors-today/#7eb5d1582f78.

CHAPTER THREE

1. David Floyd, "Cornelius Vanderbilt: Success Story," *Investopedia*, 2018, https://www.investopedia.com/university/cornelius-vanderbilt-biography/cornelius-vanderbilt-success-story.asp.

2. T. J. Stiles, "Character Spotlight: Thomas Gibbons," April 15, 2009, http://www.tjstiles.net/blog.htm?post=591727.

3. Joesph Sunde, "John D. Rockefeller: Lover of Money or Enterprise?" *Remnant Culture*, April 6, 2010, http://remnantculture.com/416-john-d-rockefeller-lover-of-money-or-enterprise.

4. Carl O'Donnell, "The Rockefellers: The Legacy of History's Richest Man," *Forbes,* July 11, 2014, https://www.forbes.com/sites/carlodonnell/2014/07/11/the-rockefellers-the-legacy-of-historys-richest-man/#359ed5213c26.

5. “The Gilded Age,” United States Senate, 2001, https://www.senate.gov/reference/reference_item/gilded_age.htm.

CHAPTER FOUR

1. T.J. Stiles. *The First Tycoon: the Epic Life of Cornelius Vanderbilt*, 249.

2. Ibid., 434.

3. Thomas E. Woods Jr., “Vanderbilt, Cornelius,” in *Exploring American History: From Colonial Times to 1877*, edited by Thomas Lansford and Thomas E. Woods, 10 (New York: Marshall Cavendish Corporation, 2008), 1051.

4. Grand By Design,” New York Transit Museum, 2014, http://gcthistory.com.

5. Christopher Gray, “Streetscapres/Grande Central Terminal; How a Rail Complex Chugged Into the 20th Century,” *New York Times*, June 21, 1998, https://www.nytimes.com/1998/06/21/realestate/streetscapes-grand-central-terminal-rail-complex-chugged-into-20th-century.html.

6. Edward J. Renehand Jr., *Commodore: the Life of Cornelius Vanderbilt* (New York: Basic Books, 2007), xii.

CHAPTER FIVE

1. John O’Sullivan, “Annexation,” *The United States Magazine and Democratic Review*, Vol. 17 (New York: 1845).

2. Charles River Editors, *American Legends: the Life of Cornelius Vanderbilt*," (Seattle, WA: Create Space Publishing, 2015).

3. Bill Carey, "Commodore Cornelius Vanderbilt Fought War Over Route Through Central America," *Vanderbilt Register*, March 11, 2002, https://news.vanderbilt.edu/archived-news/register/articles/index-id=6686.html.

4. Robert McNamara, "Cornelius Vanderbilt: 'The Commodore'," ThoughtCo, March 6, 2017, https://www.thoughtco.com/cornelius-vanderbilt-the-commodore-1773616.

CHAPTER SIX

1. Steve Fraser, "The Misunderstood Robber Baron: On Cornelius Vanderbilt," *The Nation*, November 30, 2009, https://www.thenation.com/article/misunderstood-robber-baron-cornelius-vanderbilt.

2. Robert McNamara, "Cornelius Vanderbilt: 'The Commodore'," ThoughtCo, March 6, 2017, https://www.thoughtco.com/cornelius-vanderbilt-the-commodore-1773616.

3. "The New Monopolies," *The Week*, July 28, 2017, http://theweek.com/articles/714716/new-monopolies.

4. T.J. Stiles, *The First Tycoon: the Epic Life of Cornelius Vanderbilt*, 6.

FURTHER INFORMATION

BOOKS

Carlisle, Rodeny P. *The Gilded Age: 1870 to 1900*. Handbook to Life in America. Seattle, WA: Amazon Digital Services: 2009.

Chernow, Ron. *Titan: The Life of John D. Rockefeller, Sr.* 2nd ed. New York: Random House, 2004.

Solomon, Brian. *Steam Power*. Minneapolis, MN: Voyageur Press, 2009.

Starr, Timothy. *Railroad Wars of New York State*. Charleston, NC: The History Press, 2012.

Wolmar, Christian. *The Great Railroad Revolution: The History of Trains in America*. Philadelphia, PA: Perseus Book Group, 2012.

WEBSITES

Geni: Cornelius Vanderbilt
https://www.geni.com/people/Cornelius-Vanderbilt/6000000006954317556

Explore Cornelius Vanderbilt's genealogy and relatives with Geni.

History: Cornelius Vanderbilt
https://www.history.com/topics/cornelius-vanderbilt

History.com provides a brief but engaging biography of Cornelius Vanderbilt.

National Railroad Hall of Fame: Cornelius Vanderbilt
http://www.nrrhof.org/cornelius-vanderbilt

Here, explore Vanderbilt's role in the National Railroad Hall of Fame.

Q-Files—The Great Illustrated Encyclopedia: "History of Steamships"
https://www.q-files.com/technology/ships-and-boats/history-of-steamships

This interactive website allows readers to explore and learn about steamships.

MUSEUMS

Biltmore Estate
One Lodge Street
Asheville, NC 28803

Hudson River Maritime Museum
50 Rondout Landing
Kingston, New York 12401

National Railroad Museum
2285 South Broadway
Green Bay, WI 54304

Vanderbilt Mansion, Museum, and Planetarium
180 Little Neck Road
Centerport, New York 11721

BIBLIOGRAPHY

"Andrew Jackson." Biography. Last modified 2018. https://www.biography.com/people/andrew-jackson-9350991.

"Articles of Confederation." History. Last modified 2018. https://www.history.com/topics/articles-of-confederation.

Bowles, Nellie. "The Digital Gilded Age: DC Faces Silicon Valley's Riches- and Ever-Growing Power." *Guardian*. Last modified April 17, 2016. https://www.theguardian.com/technology/2016/apr/17/zuckerberg-trump-silicon-valley-power-gilded-age.

"Cornelius Jeremiah Vanderbilt." Find a Grave. Last modified 2018. https://www.findagrave.com/memorial/90896078/cornelius-jeremiah-vanderbilt

Derbyshire, Wyn. *Six Tycoons: the Lives of John Jacob Astor, Cornelius Vanderbilt, Andrew Carnegie, John D. Rockefeller, Henry Ford, Joseph P. Kennedy*. London, UK: Spiramus Press Ltd, 2011.

Doll, Gaynelle. "Tales of the Commodore." *Vanderbilt Magazine*. Summer 1994, no. 3 (77): 6-11.

Edwards, Rebecca. "Trusts & Monopolies." Vassar.edu. Last modified 2000. http://projects.vassar.edu/1896/trusts.html.

Freidel, Frank, and Hugh Sidey. "Theodore Roosevelt." White House. Last modified 2006. https://www.whitehouse.gov/about-the-white-house/presidents/theodore-roosevelt/.

Gray, Christopher. "When Vanderbilt Did Not Get His Way." *New York Times*. Last modified September 10, 2009. http://www.nytimes.com/2009/09/13/realestate/13scapes.html.

"The Industrial Revolution in the United States." Library of Congress. Accessed March 1, 2018. http://www.loc.gov/teachers/classroommaterials/primarysourcesets/industrial-revolution/pdf/teacher_guide.pdf.

"John Fitch." Encyclopedia Britannica. Last modified February 22, 2017. https://www.britannica.com/biography/John-Fitch.

Kohlhepp, Jennifer. "Hightstown: The Trains That Once Transversed Through Town." Centraljersey.com. Last modified August 9, 2013. http://www.centraljersey.com/news/windsor_hight_herald/hightstown-the-trains-that-once-traversed-through-town/article_532ad846-f3c3-5659-8793-211d275e827e.html.

Lambert, Andrew. "A British Perspective on the War of 1812." PBS. Accessed March 6, 2018. http://www.pbs.org/wned/war-of-1812/essays/british-perspective.

Lobley, Pam. "Differences Between Wealthy, Middle Class and Poor in the Industrial Revolution." Classroom. Last modified 2018. https://classroom.synonym.com/

differences-between-wealthy-middle-class-poor-industrial-revolution-17180.html.

Long, Tony. "Aug. 17, 1807: 'Fulton's Folly' Steams Up the Hudson." Wired. Last modified August 17, 2011. https://www.wired.com/2011/08/0817robert-fulton-steamship-fultons-folly-hudson.

"Manifest Destiny." USHistory.org. Last modified 2018. http://www.ushistory.org/us/29.asp.

McNamara, Robert. "Gibbons v. Ogden." ThoughtCo. Last modified May 1, 2017. https://www.thoughtco.com/gibbons-v-ogden-4137759.

McNamara, Robert. "Jay Gould, Notorious Robber Baron." ThoughtCo. Last modified July 31, 2017. https://www.thoughtco.com/jay-gould-notorious-robber-baron-1773957.

Morris, Charles R. *The Tycoons: How Andrew Carnegie, John D. Rockefeller, Jay Gould, and J.P. Morgan Invented the American Supereconomy*. New York: Henry Holt and Company LLC, 2005.

"New York City." History. Last modified 2018. https://www.history.com/topics/new-york-city.

"New York History Timeline." I Love NY. Last modified 2018. https://www.iloveny.com/things-to-do/history/timeline.

"New York Stock Exchange (NYSE)." FXCM a Leucadia Company. Last modified 2018. https://www.fxcm.com/insights/new-york-stock-exchange-nyse.

O'Donnell, Carl. "The Legacy Of History's Richest Man." *Forbes.* Last modified July 11, 2014. https://www.forbes.com/sites/carlodonnell/2014/07/11/the-rockefellers-the-legacy-of-historys-richest-man/#5ce203a83c26.

"Overview of the Gilded Age." Digital History. Last modified 2016. http://www.digitalhistory.uh.edu/era.cfm?eraid=9.

"The Progressive Era (1890–1920). The Eleanor Roosevelt Papers Project. Accessed March 10, 2018. https://www2.gwu.edu/~erpapers/teachinger/glossary/progressive-era.cfm.

Renehan, Edward J. Jr. *Commodore: the Life of Cornelius Vanderbilt*. New York: Basic Books, 2007.

"Robert Fulton." Encyclopedia Britannica. Last modified February 17, 2018. https://www.britannica.com/biography/Robert-Fulton-American-inventor.

Stiles, T.J. "Character Spotlight: Thomas Gibbons." T.J. Stiles. Last modified August 15, 2009. http://www.tjstiles.net/blog.htm?post=591727

———. "The Commodore's Civil War." *Vanderbilt Magazine.* Last modified April 11, 2011. https://news.vanderbilt.edu/vanderbiltmagazine/the-commodores-civil-war.

———. *The First Tycoon: the Epic Life of Cornelius Vanderbilt.* New York: Vintage Books, 2010.

"Table 2, Population of 24 Urban Places: 1790." Census.gov. Accessed: March 1, 2018. https://www.census.gov/population/www/documentation/twps0027/tab02.txt.

"Thomas Alexander Scott." Your Dictionary. Accessed March 4, 2018. http://biography.yourdictionary.com/thomas-alexander-scott.

"Thomas Newcomen (1663–1729.)" BBC.com. Last modified 2014. http://www.bbc.co.uk/history/historic_figures/newcomen_thomas.shtml.

"Via Nicaragua Private Mail Route." RFRAJola.com. Accessed March 8, 2018. http://www.rfrajola.com/overland%20routes/OM15.pdf.

Young, Michelle. "A Guide to the Gilded Age Mansions of 5th Avenue's Millionaire Row." 6sqft. Last modified August 22, 2017. https://www.6sqft.com/a-guide-to-the-gilded-age-mansions-of-5th-avenues-millionaire-row.

INDEX

Page numbers in **boldface** refer to images.

ABOUT THE AUTHOR

Cassandra Schumacher has a background in anthropology and creative writing with a focus in cultural and historical studies. Schumacher's interests are vast and varied but predominately focus on the study of human and cultural identity throughout history into modern times. Much of her writing focuses on socio-cultural interactions and power dynamics, and seeks to explore a holistic understanding of a variety of concepts and topics relating to human history. Schumacher's work most especially studies post-revolutionary American history as well as some ethnographic studies of other regions.